ATHEIST, FRIEND OR FOE?

What Christians Should Know

LOUIS PERRY

ISBN: 1503127567
ISBN 13: 9781503127562
Library of Congress Control Number: 2014920063
CreateSpace Independent Publishing Platform
North Charleston, South Carolina

CONTENTS

Acknowledgments

Much thanks to the informative and lively discussions with Reverend Laurel Gray, a retired Lutheran minister, and his group of Progressive Christians. Their efforts bring an understanding of the biblical narrative and Jesus' message into context with modernity as presented by advances in natural science and secular governance laws. Their efforts give hope of reducing the conflicts between Christianity, natural science and our democracy.

PROLOGUE

IN A COUNTRY with religious freedom, why do some Christians today believe Atheists should be considered foes and attacked? Are not Atheists and other non-believers also Americans who differ only in their beliefs—as believers of all other religions do? Why then are Atheists singled out, labeled, and attacked as being more subversive than believers of other religions?

This is an old action by Christians, who, history reveals, have been attacking Atheists from the beginning of Christianity, some two thousand years ago. Yet they are both still around and increasing in numbers. Today there are 1.2 billion or so Christians tussling with a very much smaller number of Atheists, who are relatively disorganized, are not in many positions of power, and have no organizations of significant size, but continue to slowly grow in numbers. Why not just let Atheists continue to stumble along their path to hell, dazzled by their affinity for Nature?

The answer from many Christians is that the Atheist view is a threat—they think Nature (not God) is the creator of humans and the universe. They think human morals are not given from God on high, but partly inherited from ancestors and partly learned after birth. This secular base for Atheism is difficult for some Christians to accept. The role of faith, after all, is very different from non-faith—so much so that it is unsettling to some Christians. As the biology professor Jerry Coyne notes,

In religion faith is a virtue. In science faith is a vice.

The differences between religion and natural science are vast, and it is obvious the two cannot be mixed without conflicts arising. Therefore, the two must be separated for either to excel as a discipline. Christians have long answered the question of how to treat Atheists: when in political power call Atheists foes and run them out of town; when not in power tolerate them and when in a time of crisis solicit their help. This has been the case for over two thousand years and for some Christians it remains the case today.

Some militant Christians believe they must continue the fight against Atheists to resist three factors they believe are harming Christianity:

> 1) The expanding acceptance of secular scientific advances that point to Nature as the creator and designer of the universe and humans.
>
> 2) The expanding acceptance of liberal social positions regarding marriage, contraception, homosexuality, and others that conflict with a Fundamentalist reading of the Bible.
>
> 3) The emergence of Progressive Christians who have begun to adjust their views of the nature of God, accept the advances of natural science, and accept Atheists.

Interestingly, Atheism has not been and is not today one of the major problems facing Christians in the competitive world of religions. Larger problems have come from the internal fissures within Christianity. There is diversity inherent in the spectrum of any religion and Christianity is no different. Individual Christian believers each seek a better understand of their God so there are many views of God within Christianity. It is the difference from this diversity that causes these rifts. This quest for true belief has birthed numerous Christian denominations with different views of Christianity's very core. This only adds to the confusion and defensiveness of many Christians, each of which holds to their belief that only they know the real nature of God.

In the following discussions the world is divided into two domains: Nature, one that obeys the laws of Nature which are discovered by repeatable observations and experiments and the second is God, one defined by a supernatural narrative invented by man in which it is not necessary to obey the laws of Nature, but does have laws to obey from the narrative. In short there is the domain of Nature in which we run experiments to try and understand and the domain of the Christian God which is accepted by belief. Other godly domains are not discussed. The Nature domain must be kept separate from the God domain for if mixed the domain of Nature also becomes supernatural and the integrity of natural science lost.

Conflicts arise when Christians choose the "truths" of their supernatural biblical narrative over scientific "truths." Atheists see a workable solution by considering the biblical passages which conflict with natural science as supernatural metaphors. Separating the supernatural in the Christian narrative from natural science allows views of both domains—one, Nature described by natural science which forbids the supernatural, andthe second, God, described by the biblical narrative which incorporates the supernatural.

The world around Christians has and will continue to change over time and impart new conflicts from the advances of scientific theories, philosophies, and social mores. Attacking Atheists as a primary cause of these real-world changes has been the de facto solution by Christians for two thousand years, but with today's expanded availability of information and ease of fact-checking, Christian attacks on Atheists reveal a lack of factual support and expose old falsehoods used for labeling Atheists as evildoers.

To shed some light on the depth, breadth, and soundness of the attacks continuing on Atheists, the writings of two Christian apologists are examined in regard to their acceptance or non-acceptance of the advances in natural science, social mores, and the secular laws of our American democracy. Belief in a God and a religion is a personal freedom all Americans enjoy, but attacking believers and non-believers is an action worthy of comment. Further, by studying the attacks, one can develop insights into how to expose and/or avoid them. Religious insight is provided by studying the beliefs of Progressive Christians who have learned to honor the strengths of both Christianity and natural science and live with the known differences.

INTRODUCTION

THE ADVERSARIAL ARGUMENTS by Fundamentalist Christians against Atheists and natural science have been documented in the writings and teachings of many Christian apologists. This study will focus on two books from well-known Fundamentalist writers. Both provide examples of the attacks. The books are *What's So Great about Christianity?*, by Dinesh D'Souza and *The Face of Atheism*, by Ravi Zacharias. D'Souza is the ex-president of a small Christian college and a right-wing political ideologue, and Zacharias is a popular evangelical minister. Their books are representative of the anti-Atheist and anti–natural science tone of current Fundamentalist Christians. Their attacks shed light on Christian ideology of the majority religion in America, and on the ideology of Atheism, a much smaller group. . Somehow the attacking Christians find it acceptable to ignore the religious freedom the Constitution grants to all religions, including Atheism.

Today, demonizing Atheists is mostly accomplished by the far right of the Christian spectrum (Fundamentalist Christians). They routinely accuse Atheists of many evil things that are actually the very things Fundamentalist Christians are struggling with in the modern world: the natural science of creation and evolution of the universe and humans, the medical science of human reproduction and abortion, the liberalization of social laws, the enforcement of laws relating to the separation of church and state, and the use of only natural science in public education. In essence, Atheists are blamed for all the problems Fundamentalists Christians are having with modernity.

Modernity includes the acceptance of natural science's description of the universe and man and the acceptance of many religions' supernatural narratives. Science is not antireligion, for religions are based on supernatural beliefs that science does not address. Science does not attempt to get rid of religion, but it does attempt to keep religion from stepping on science's turf—that is, ensuring that science's "truths" are not trumped by supernatural religious "truths," for they are separate.

Of course, not all Christians are Fundamentalists. Christian beliefs cover a widely diverse spectrum in terms of accepting Atheism and natural science. Three Christian groups will be used as examples: Fundamentalists, Moderates, and Progressives. Fundamentalists believe in a supernatural God that is omnipotent and one that has created the universe and man. This is the God of D'Souza and Zacharias. They are about a quarter of all Christians, and they believe the supernatural Bible should be read literally and their God has authority over natural science and governmental laws.

Moderates, the largest group, have developed some acceptance of science, but they believe God controls Nature. They consider the Bible the inspired word of God but believe it does contain some errors. The Progressives, the smallest group, accept natural science as an independent discipline and view the Bible as a human-written book that contains both history and interpretations of history told metaphorically in stories.

Although Moderates talk about accepting natural science, such as Darwin's Theory and the Big Bang theory, their acceptance falls short of embracing the resulting implications of the natural science theories. For example, Darwin's Theory of natural selection precludes the sudden appearance of Adam and Eve, one fully formed pair of Homo sapiens, from which all humans evolved. Rather, it requires a string of millions of mating pairs from the first common ancestor on to our ancestors in the Homo sapiens branch of the tree of life. With many evolving ancestral pairs, there was no one couple that committed the Original Sin. Other Moderates (including Deists) see God as having started the universe but having only limited interactions with humanity afterward.

The third and smallest group, the Progressive Christians, accepts Atheists' view of science and holds to a non-literal reading of the supernatural biblical narrative. For example, the Adam and Eve story is considered to be a metaphor for introducing mankind's sins, as are other parts of the narrative, and therefore not in conflict with natural science.

At this end of the spectrum are Unitarians, who accept science and a broad spirituality that includes Christianity but is not limited by it. Then there are the Agnostics (those who cannot decide whether there is a God or not) and the Atheists. Atheists accept natural science and reject a supernatural God, but accept the religious beliefs of others in whatever God they wish as long as it doesn't encroach on Nature or the secular government.

This book puts forward the views of Atheists and their positions on natural science, governance and religion, including the genesis of gods. Readers with different views on their God from that offered by Atheists are free to adjust the arguments accordingly for the belief in a God is a deeply personal belief decision.

1

ATHEISTS

ATHEISTS AND THEIR Deist, Unitarian, and Agnostic cousins are not new groups invading the Christian world. In fact, as long as there have been theists, there have been Atheists. Theists believe there is a supernatural God described by a supernatural religious story explaining the creation of the universe and humanity. Atheists also try to explain the mysterious universe around them, but they find that Nature better answers the questions of the creation of the universe and humans. They also hold that humans evolved with the intellectual capabilities to create supernatural stories of religions with gods. In short, they thank Nature for giving us an understanding of human evolution and the emergence of stories of supernatural gods.

According to natural science, modern humans (*Homo sapiens*) evolved from earlier primate ancestors some two hundred thousand years ago. It can even be argued that all our ancestors were Atheists. There is no indication of gods until about fifty thousand years ago, as can best be gleaned from the sketchy artifacts found. These indicate that humans began about that time to invent supernatural gods, recite spiritual narratives, illustrate cave walls with art, and construct spiritual gathering places for their tribes. Since then many gods have been invented all around the world. In the West there have been supernatural stories about Egyptian gods, Persian gods, Greek gods, Roman gods, Jewish gods, and many other gods. Judaism transformed from polytheism to monotheism about three thousand years ago, and about two thousand years ago, Jesus was born and began the emergence of Christianity from Judaism. In the East other gods in other religions, such as Hinduism, Jainism, and Taoism, were invented.

After the rise of Christianity, Christians won the theocratic power struggle within the all-powerful Roman Empire in AD 325, and Christianity became the dominant religion in the subsequent ruling theocracies. Their success led to extending their power to other countries, and Christian theocracies governed in the Western world for most of the next 1,500 years. Atheists, with their belief in Nature instead of a supernatural God, survived in the shadows of Christianity.

From the beginning of Christianity, there was great effort by denominations to define a uniform religious dogma and then enforce believer conformity to that dogma. For a thousand years, the Roman Catholic theocracies succeeded in holding the power to enforce their dogmas, but that changed as the Church grew very large and control of the expanded priesthood became nearly impossible from their diversity of interests. Priests began worrying about whether they really understood God and about whether the dogma supported their beliefs. From all this new thought, suggestions of change to some of the Church's dogma arose and reformation of the Church began.

Jan Hus, a Czech priest and philosopher, began to question one dogma—indulgencies (money raised for the Church for directed prayers). However, the Church strongly defended its dogma, and the resulting confrontation in 1415 ended with Hus being burned at the stake for his attempts. A hundred years later, another priest, Martin Luther, called for a similar change in Germany. This time the confrontation with the Vatican created a spark within the priests and lay persons that went further and started the Protestant Reformation. This split the Church and led not only to Protestant churches but to ruling Protestant theocracies in a number of European countries.

During this time, Atheism and other religious views remained at the margins and in the shadows, for the existence of a supernatural God in charge of everything was not challenged. The secular Enlightenment changed that, though. Atheists and Deists philosophers suddenly began to be accepted into mainstream philosophy, and it became possible, if not still dangerous, to talk about secular governments that did not have religion in a dominant position of power and recognize that the people as the source of governmental power. Even the limitations of God's power and God's agents, the kings, in governing could be discussed.

By the time of the American Revolution, there was already an expanding secular philosophical base in Europe and America. The Founding Fathers openly discussed personal freedoms, power of the citizens, and separating governments from religion. Thus, in America when drafting the Declaration of Independence, Thomas Jefferson could be independent of Christian dogma, refer to the *"Laws of Nature and of Nature's God,"* and be acceptable to the deistic philosophy that had support among many of his fellow delegates. The Declaration was signed unanimously, and subsequently, the Constitution was ratified by a congress that had a majority of Christians without reference to the Christian God. The Americans had taken a major step toward separating the government from religion. That Constitution still governs America.

Early Beliefs

Myths and religion employing supernatural gods have been an important factor in humanity's development. Bronislaw Malinowski[1] has argued:

> *"Myth fulfills in primitive culture an indispensable function: it expresses, enhances, and codifies*

— 3 —

belief, it safeguards and enforces morality, it vouches for the efficiency of ritual and contains practical rules for the guidance of man." Myths achieve this social function, he observed, by serving as guides, or charters, for moral values, social order and magical belief. "Myth is thus a vital ingredient of human civilization; it is not an idle tale, but a hard-worked active force; it is not an intellectual explanation or an artistic imagery, but a pragmatic charter of primitive faith and moral wisdom."

The inventiveness of man ensured that there were many myths and gods to choose from. There were also doubters, the Atheists, who asked why this god or that god? Further the Atheists asked the early religions the question, is there a need for a supernatural god? Can we not find the answers in Nature.

Atheists are at one end of the belief spectrum. They say there is no need for a supernatural God to explain the world. Rather, one can learn from Nature. Several early philosophers cogently expressed this view. The Greek philosopher Epicurus famously did so in the third century BC, and the Roman philosopher Lucretius poetically built on his work in the first century AD. They argued that only Nature or Nature's God was needed to explain the world. Nature could speak for itself. According to Epicurus,

There is no god or any other agent standing outside of nature that can explain why the things within it are one way and not another. Nature acts according to causes, not purposes.

Several hundred years later, Lucretius expanded upon the same philosophy:

Nature is her own mistress and is exempt from the oppression of arrogant despots accomplishing everything by herself spontaneously and independently and free from the jurisdiction of the gods.

— 4 —

But *"the jurisdiction of the gods"* did come after the Roman Emperor Constantine accepted Christianity into the Roman Empire in AD 325 and the Western world began to be governed by Christian theocracies. A series of powerful Christian theocracies succeeded in becoming the governmental norm throughout the Western world for the next thousand years. During this time the earlier Atheist and Deist philosophies by Epicurus, Lucretius, and others remained attractive to some Christians, but the Christian Church labeled those so inclined as heretics and persecuted them. The Epicurean philosophy managed to survive only by remaining quietly in the shadows of Christian theocracies.

A few hundred years after the ascendancy of Christianity in the Roman Empire, militant Christians were directed to eliminate the Atheists, pagans, and heretics throughout the Roman Empire. One of the most infamous killings occurred in AD 415, when a Christian street mob killed Hypatia, a renowned pagan teacher, scholar, and scientist in Alexandria. Her death and other such killings greatly impacted not only the world-renown learning center in Alexandria but many other centers of learning throughout the Empire.

For the next 1,300 years, Atheists continued to be declared enemies of Christian theocracies and were killed or forced underground as outcasts. However, some of their literature has survived. One example is in the *Carmina Burana*, which clergy and students wrote around 1200. It is a collection of poems and music that contains references to bawdy vagabond songs and poems of Epicurus. These poems were included in a copy of the *Carmina Burana* that was later found in 1803 in a Christian abbey in Germany. Atheists survived by hiding their views, but in some cases, they were caught and put to death.

In the background, some priests continued to explore different views on the nature of God and other dogmas of Christianity. This included the validity of the Holy Trinity—a concept that emerged after AD 100. Priest and scientist

Michael Servetus questioned this concept in his book published in 1551, *On the Errors of the Trinity*. Catholics and Protestants alike condemned this book. While he was in Geneva, Servetus corresponded with John Calvin on his views and his book. This encounter led to his arrest and death by Protestants who burned him at the stake in 1553. A small group of Christians who argued for the need for more religious tolerance for differing views within the Christian community thought his death unnecessarily harsh. This group later became known as Unitarians.

From the seventeenth century onward, as more knowledge of Nature emerged from scientific advancesa few Christians increasingly questioned the Christian dogma on the nature of the universe. Within the Catholic Church, several priests were attracted to the Epicurean concept of an infinite universe.

Another priest, Giordano Bruno, traveled widely and wrote about the infinite universe concept from Epicurus's philosophy. His book *Universe and World* was published in 1584 and caught the attention of the Vatican, for it directly conflicted with the Church's dogma of a fixed universe with the Earth and humanity at the center. For writing his book and speaking on the subject, Bruno was accused of being an Atheist and heretic and thrown into jail. After seven years, in 1600, he was burned at the stake in Rome. With the passing of time, advancing science has boosted Bruno's views as did the publication of Copernicus's heliocentric theory, the cosmic observations of Galileo using his new telescope, and Kepler's publication of more accurate theories of planetary motion contributed to the understanding of the universe.

A few years later, another Italian priest, Lucilio Vanini, made a name for himself as "*that ringleader of the atheists*" with the publication of several books supporting Epicurean concepts. He was also one of the first to argue that humans evolved from apes. In *On the Wonderful Secrets of Nature, the Queen and Goddess of Mortal Beings,* he argued for the existence of a God many said could not be distinguished from Nature. The Church accused him of not being an orthodox Christian, labeled him an Atheist, and jailed and put him to death in France in 1619.

With the emergence of the secular Enlightenment in the eighteenth century, European societies began to change and become more tolerant, liberal, and supportive of advances in natural science and philosophy. The increasing knowledge of Nature began to attract several philosophers who questioned the theocratic power of governments and the natures of God but not the existence of God. The early seventeenth-century philosopher Thomas Hobbes introduced the precept of a social contract for governments—the view that all legitimate political power must be "representative" and based on the consent of the people. He was also a biblical scholar and is usually credited with launching a rationalistic approach to reading the Bible. His studies led him to argue that Moses did not write the first five books of the Old Testament. Opponents of his philosophy called him an Atheist, but he defended himself against such charges.

Later in the century in 1650 the Dutch and Jewish philosopher Bernard Spinoza was kicked out of his synagogue for his arguments supporting science and against supernatural miracles by saying,

> *Whatever we clearly and distinctly understand must become known to us either through itself or through some other thing that is clearly and distinctly understood through itself. Therefore from a miracle, or an event that surpasses our understanding, we can understand nothing.*

Spinoza, however, went even further:

> *To conceive God as issuing commands, answering prayers, permitting miracles, is to be swayed*

by superstition. The Bible is but an historical compilation that could not possibly be written by those it claims.

Spinoza then paid tribute to moral messages of Jesus:

We might rightly admire some moral messages, but there is no reason to think the Bible contains philosophical truths. Understanding Scripture is to understand man-made historical documents.

The philosophical tide of the Enlightenment was beginning to openly embrace reason and Nature and accept a picture of a less expansive and authoritative God. Spinoza also argued for the study of the Bible as one would study any other historical document. In his reasoning, the value of the Torah was as a constitution for the early State of Israel, but since that state no longer existed, it should not be considered generally applicable today.

Led by Spinoza (the "Atheist Jew") and John Locke, the concept of God in the Enlightenment began to embrace the Deists' view: God started the universe but afterward had little interactive relationship with humanity. God was referred to as a "watchmaker God"—the God who built the universe and set it running. Locke also stated that true revelation can never be in disagreement with human reason and experience.

However, the scientific and philosophical successes continued to fight an uphill battle for acceptance by the established Christian theocracies. These theocracies continued to defend the biblical narrative with its pseudo-science dogmas. Supporters of new scientific theories were still called Atheists or heretics, and some were killed for their views. However, society's increased acceptance of the new philosophy began to diminish the Church's power to put them to death for their views. Still, the linking of Atheists with evil attacks on dogma had been etched into the folklore.

Enlightenment

At the beginning of the American Revolution, there were a number of philosophers in Europe and America embracing the Enlightenment philosophy. Matthew Stewart notes:

> *Locke is regarded as the single most important philosophical influence on America's revolutionary leaders. Locke and Spinoza are the chalk and cheese of the early Enlightenment, or so it has long been maintained. One was moderate in all things; the other a thoroughgoing radical. One was supposedly a devout follower of Jesus; the other was known in his own day as "the atheist Jew."*

Another philosopher was Immanuel Kant, who helped bring philosophy and natural science together to form a base for understanding Nature. Concerning philosophy, Kant said:

> *Using reason [to develop philosophy] without applying it to experience only leads to theoretical illusions.*

This procedure is comparable to the scientific process, which dictates that using reason to develop theories without experimental verification leads only to theoretical illusions. This philosophy is essentially that of the scientific community. It requires that theories developed by reason be supported by experimental proof to be accepted as theories describing Nature.

In defining their new state, Americans had a number of philosophers to call upon—Alexander Pope, David Hume, Lord Bolingbroke, and Joseph Priestley from England, Voltaire from France, John Toland from Ireland, and Ethan Allen, Thomas Paine, and Thomas Young from America. Jefferson's library included all these philosophers and more in a category he labeled "moral philosophy." Both Jefferson and Benjamin Franklin held discussions on the philosophy of personal freedoms and power of the people also with some of these philosophers while traveling in Europe.

These philosophical discussions and books converted Franklin into a Deist, and Franklin was not alone. Early on in the American Revolution, Reverend Nathan Perkins pilloried Ethan Allen, the hero of Ticonderoga, for being a Deist. Perkins declared Allen to be

> *an awful infidel, one of ye wickedest men yet ever*
> *walked this guilty globe.*

Perkins reported with dismay in 1789 that there were many Americans in this same category:

> *About one quarter of the inhabitants and almost*
> *all of the men of learning [are] deists.*

As the diversity of Christian belief broadened from the secular influence, many Christian intellectuals in England and America, including some of the Founding Fathers,[2] were called Atheists or Deists. They generally acknowledged that God might have started the infinite universe in motion, but he was not necessary afterward. The Englishman Richard Bentley captured the philosophical mood of that period and complained that

> *"The modern disguised Deists...do cover the most*
> *arrant atheism under the mask and shadow of*
> *a deity, by which they understand no more than*
> *some eternal inanimate matter, some universal*
> *nature, and soul of the world.*

The Christian spectrum widened further in England and America to include those who were more tolerant, more liberal and rejected some Christian doctrines such as the Holy Trinity. These people became Unitarians.

At the time of the American Revolution, the nation had a Christian majority but with a strong cadre of Atheists, Deists, and Unitarians playing critical roles. In many cases, they were the leading radicals behind the fight for independence from England. Author Matthew Stewart[3] sets the stage:

*In the years preceding the Revolutionary War, it
should not be forgotten, only a tiny fraction of the
American colonials desired independence, and
only a much smaller fraction thought in terms of
a democratic transformation of society and government. [Thomas] Young belonged to a numeri-
cally insignificant sliver who, long before their
fellow colonials dared to imagine the possibility
of a break from the mother country, dreamed of
independence as a means to launch a democratic
revolution that would sweep through the British
Empire and then around the world.*

That small sliver of Americans (the Atheists, Deists, and
Unitarians) involved in the Revolution included many famil-
iar names. Randall Balmer at Columbia University noted
that:

*religious belief at this time was a product of
the age and class, that was inebriated with the
Enlightenment rationalism.*

To many Christians, the Atheists, Deists, and Unitarians had
all deviated from orthodox Christianity and for these differences in views, they were called "Atheists." Key Revolutionary
heroes among this group include the following:

Ethan Allen—Sometimes listed as the forgotten
Founding Father, he led the Green Mountain Boys
from Vermont and captured the British strong-
hold of Fort Ticonderoga in 1775. This was an
important boost to believing independence from
Britain could be achieved. He was also a leader for
statehood of Vermont.

He later wrote *The Oracles of Reason*. This was an
attack on the Christian clergy, whom he thought
would present a problem for the new country when
separating from the British government and its
state religion. His book was influential at a critical

time leading up to the Revolution. However, after the Revolution, it elicited a strong but expected backlash from mainline Christians. They used this book to remove him from the public eye.

Thomas Young—At twenty-five he was charged and found guilty of blasphemy for his Deist views. A few years later, he was one of the originators of the Boston Tea Party. Young came before the assembled people of Boston on November 29, 1773, and outlined the illegal tax proposition and proposed dumping the East India Company's cargo into the harbor. He was the only one at the Tea Party not in an Indian disguise, and shortly afterward, the British easily arrested him. They almost killed him for participating in the affair.

Thomas Paine—His principal contribution was the powerful and widely read pamphlet *Common Sense*. It was released on the timely date of January 1776. John Adams, the second president, noted its importance: "*Without the pen of the author of* Common Sense, *the sword of Washington would have been raised in vain.*"

In May 1776, Paine, Young, and a handful of their fellow radicals were instrumental in replacing the legitimately elected government of the province with a pro-independence faction. This faction tilted the balance of the Continental Congress in favor of permanent separation from Britain, and within six weeks, the congress declared independence.

In 1793 he published the *Age of Reason*, in which he argued that Christianity and all other religions were human inventions. He advocated Deism, promoted reason, and was one of the first in the new country to be called an Atheist for not being

Christian enough. Eighty years later, this view of Paine was still around when Teddy Roosevelt called him

a dirty, little atheist.

Over the years, however, history has revealed his vital contributions to the American Revolutionary cause, and today he is considered a Revolutionary hero who happens to have been an Atheist.

Thomas Jefferson—Jefferson was a young delegate to the Continental Congress from Virginia when John Adams urged a committee of the congress to ask Jefferson to write the Declaration of Independence. He wrote a draft in 1776. Benjamin Franklin reviewed it and submitted it to the congress for approval and signing. The Continental Congress unanimously signed the Declaration on July 4, 1776.

In the document, Jefferson referenced "*the Laws of Nature and of Nature's God.*" Stewart notes this

properly belongs to the radical philosophical religion of deism. It refers to nothing that we commonly mean by the term "God," but rather to something closer to "Nature." It tells us that we are and always have been the source of our own authority.

Religious freedom had been a major interest of Jefferson's from the time he was a young member of the Virginia legislature. During that time, he introduced the Virginia Statute for Religious Freedom. This disestablished the Church of England in Virginia and guaranteed the freedom of religion to people of all faiths—Protestants, Catholics, and Jews. It took seven years to get the statute passed, and that was only after help from James Madison. Jefferson later worked closely with

Madison to ensure the concept of the separation of church and state was embedded in the First Amendment of the Constitution.

Jefferson was a brilliant, complex man with many talents. Although he gave money to churches, he almost never went to church, and several opponents called him an Atheist while he was in public service. He was twice elected president. He was a curious scholar who collected books and assembled the largest library in the country.

He studied all the philosophy books he could obtain. He placed the Bible in the category of moral philosophy and studied it for many years. He thought Jesus offered profound morals that he should add to his personal cache. He edited the Bible by cutting out those passages he thought were the profound moral teachings of Jesus, and he pasted them in a little book he called *The Life and Morals of Jesus of Nazareth Extracted Textually from the Gospels in Greek, Latin, French and English.*[4] The book is also known as *The Jefferson Bible.* (See appendix C, Notes on *The Jefferson Bible.*)

Many called Jefferson an Atheist and at other times a Deist, but in public he would only say he was a denomination of one. His philosophy did include Epicurus's idea that the source of happiness was to grasp the form and reason of Nature. He expressed this thought throughout his life. In one heated exchange with his friend John Adams, Adams replied,

Ye will say I am no Christian: I say Ye are no Christian.

After retiring from the presidency, he founded the University of Virginia. This was the first secular university in the country and one without a theology department. Jefferson held the new university to be one of his three achievements worthy of being placed on his tombstone. The other two were authoring the Virginia Statue for Religious Freedom and the Declaration of Independence. These three efforts alone place Jefferson as a major force to effect the separation of religion from government in the new country.

Many presidents, including Abraham Lincoln, considered the Declaration of Independence to be the foundation of the political philosophy of the country. It is ironic that the Declaration of Independence, written by one whom many called an Atheist, is the statement of the basic moral principles embedded in the Constitution.

James Madison—Madison, Alexander Hamilton, and John Jay wrote *The Federalist*—sixty-five essays that helped gained widespread support for the American Revolution. Madison was a Deist and a strong advocate for religious freedom and the separation of church and state. He pursued this while in the Virginia state assembly and later as a leader in the Continental Congress's drafting of the Constitution. He is the so-called Father of the Constitution, and he championed for the power of the people:

> *The people are the only legitimate fountain of power...not only that all power should be derived from the people; but, that those entrusted with it should be kept in dependence on the people.*

In the First Amendment to the Constitution, he ensured that the concept of the separation of church and state was included:

> *Congress shall make no law respecting an establishment of religion, or prohibiting the free exercise thereof.*

Other Atheists, Deists, and Unitarians—Benjamin Franklin, George Washington, and John Adams were Deists and leaders in the American Revolution. They supported local churches as a useful way to contribute to the community even though they were among the many Reverend Nathan Perkins referred to when he reported that

> *almost all of the men of learning [are] deists.*

A few months before he died, Benjamin Franklin reflected on his beliefs and wrote that he thought the

> *system of morals [given by Jesus of Nazareth] were the best the World ever saw.*

However, Franklin said he had, "*[along] with most of the present Dissenters in England, some Doubts as to his Divinity,*"

> *tho' it is a Question I do not dogmatise upon, having never studied it, and think it needless to busy myself with it now, when I expect soon an opportunity of knowing the truth with less trouble.*

This view is essentially Jefferson's. Thus, the two leading intellectuals among the Founding Fathers were Deists or more likely called Atheists for questioning the divinity of Jesus.

At the time America was founded, the majority of the people were Christians, but there was also a strong segment of Atheists, Deists, and Unitarians. The country they forged together was secular by design, for it had to ensure the freedom of religion for all. The Founding Fathers were aware of the religious strife that had ravaged European countries for centuries, and they wished to avoid having an established religion in the new country. This required a secular country with religious freedom, and it was this vision that brought Christians, Atheists, Deists, Unitarians, and others to join together in a partnership that won the struggle for independence.

The Enlightenment continued in the nineteenth century as new science theories appeared. This included Darwinian evolution in biology and theories of an ancient Earth in geology. The following 20th century introduced new scientific theories, such as the Big Bang theory of the universe's creation in cosmology and the biological evolution of morality in neuroscience. These new theories continued support of the Epicurean philosophy of Nature's universe that

Nature is her own mistress...and free from the jurisdiction of the gods.

In history Atheists have played many roles in science, art, philosophy, and government. Only in a religious community does a person label another an Atheist, and it is quite a stretch that all these millions of Atheists were evildoers. This labeling applied by Christians is an old, leftover religious belief that couples the absence of belief in a supernatural God with a presence of evil. This coupling had no validity two thousand years ago and has none today.

As with any other groupings of people around a belief, there is a spectrum of non-believers. Atheists can be bad people, good people, and all permutations between. At one end of the spectrum is a small group called militant Atheists. They are vocal against religion and see it as an evil, but most Atheists are just interested in finding "truth" about Nature rather than having it given to them from a supernatural God on high.

Although today most Christians tolerate Atheists, the old bias against them remains. When asked if they would vote for an Atheist for public office, most Christians would place an Atheist last on their lists. Being labeled "evil" in the eyes of Christians for two thousand years continues to be a hard label to remove.

Christians are not alone in attacking Atheists. It is common to all religions. Muslim extremists have made a lot of headlines across the world by attacking whom they consider to be heretics and Atheists. This work, however, deals with trying to understand why Christians attack Atheists. That is a large enough task.

Why attack Atheists in America now? Are the advances in natural science and the philosophies of Epicurus and Lucretius too threatening today? For most of history, non-believers or non-theists have been only a small percentage of the population. However, today that is changing. The number of non-theists, which includes Atheists, Deists, Agnostics, and Unitarians, is approaching a fifth of the population. That is true even in America, a religiously inclined country, and more so in many European countries. A 2014 poll[5] found that 42 percent of Americans believed God created humans in their present form ten thousand years ago, and 31 percent believed humans evolved with God's guidance. Those who believed God had no part in humans' creation were 19 percent. That 19 percent represents a doubling of non-believers and Atheists over the last twenty-five years. Among academics[6] 73 percent of philosophers said they accepted or were inclined to Atheism, while 15 percent accepted or were inclined to theism. Only around 6 percent identified themselves as Agnostics. Could this rapid increase in non-believers be one of the reasons for the attacks from Christians today?

Many Fundamentalist Christians continue to resist accepting the advances of natural science and have chosen to remain with the old, outdated Christian pseudo-science. They believe supernatural "truths" are superior in all cases to natural "truths," even though there is now an overwhelming accumulation of data supporting the natural science theories. This polarization of beliefs has led to an adversarial approach from both sides at times.

Although the numbers are small, there is now a group known as Progressive Christians, who emphasize a scholarly understanding of a metaphoric reading of the supernatural passages in the Christian narrative, believe their religion should be separate from natural science, and believe both religion and science are important to society. They seek to promote an understanding of Progressive Christianity and natural science.

2

THE BOOKS

CHRISTIAN LABELING OF Atheists as evildoers has a long history. The current visions of Atheists from Fundamentalist Christians are taken from the writings of two leading Christian apologists—Dinesh D'Souza and Ravi Zacharias. They attack Atheists and the subjects identified with Atheists and their theories. This includes natural science in general, Darwin's Theory of natural selection, the Big Bang theory, contemporary morality, secular democracy, and secular public education. Interestingly, both authors attack the same general mix of subjects. Their books remind readers that the old labels regarding Atheists as evildoers are still around, and these authors put them on display.

For this discussion, direct quotes are taken from the arguments by D'Souza and Zacharias, and specific comments are attached to each quote in reply. The use of multiple quotes (thirty-eight for D'Souza and twenty-nine for Zacharias) captures the breadth of their views on Atheists and allows a comparison of what their attacks have in common.

These two books represent the views of two Christians on Atheists. An opposite comparison (an Atheist's view of Christians), can be found in the *The Jefferson Bible*—a book assembled by Thomas Jefferson on the philosophy of Jesus. Many of

Jefferson's opponents called him an Atheist while president, so it is interesting to see the real face of Christian philosophy he captures in his book.

Comments on quotes from both books are given. D'Souza's quotes (labeled "D'S Quote") and Zacharias's quotes (labeled "Z Quote") are in italics. Answering comments (labeled "Comment") follow each quote in normal type.

Quotes from both writers and the associated comments are grouped by the subjects they attack. A summary of the comments from both books follows. This approach entails some overlap of their views, but keeping the authors' quotes and comments separate is important in retaining the identity of each author's overall philosophy. Several appendixes add depth to some important subjects, and key reference books supporting the comments are noted to provide background source material.

D'Souza's Book

The Christian apologist author Dinesh D'Souza is not a scientist or minister. He is an English major who readily engages in science-religion-democracy debates as an advocate for Fundamentalist Christian ideology. He has been around a few years writing books, debating scientists and philosophers, and most recently making movies reflecting his position as a champion of conservative Christian political ideology.

One of his books, *What's So Great about Christianity?*, directly addresses what he perceives as the Atheists' evils being inflicted on Christendom. The evils he highlights are the increasing number of Atheists, the success of natural science (what he calls "*atheist science*") with its secular theories, the lack of morals, and the introduction of liberal social issues to the American public. He blames Atheists for conducting a war against Christendom in which Atheists—"*cowardly*," in his words—use the advances of natural science, secular philosophy, secular governance, and secular public education to inflict their views on Christians. D'Souza bemoans the loss of Christian authority over the creation story of humans and the universe. To counter this string of what he calls "*atheist successes,*" he directs his attacks at Atheists, scientists, and educators, whom he holds to be the central forces diminishing Christian authority today.

D'Souza is also known from the publicity surrounding his attacks on Barack Obama during Obama's run for the presidency. These attacks were contained in his book *The Roots of Obama's Rage* and an accompanying movie, *2016: Obama's America.* His efforts were directed toward supporting the conservative political goal of defeating whom he believed to be the more liberal and less Christian Obama. However, his efforts failed. Obama won his first presidential election and a second term in the following presidential election.

Approach

The literary approach D'Souza uses in his attack on Atheists is to present usually assertions (such as "Atheists are conducting a war against Christendom") and then embellished the assertions with arguments that might or might not coincide with any truth. Natural science theories are routinely violated in his arguments, for he has no respect for the scientific community. His goal is to pin labels on Atheists as evildoers who are harming Christendom regardless of the facts. It is the same approach many salespeople over the years have used: assert that the competitor's product is terrible and/or dangerous and yours is wonderful, and then give twenty reasons why. Facts are optional.

D'Souza's non-fact-based assertions are then woven into a fictional tale favorable to his conservative Christian ideology. This leaves little question that his book is fiction based on invented and unfounded assertions aimed to achieve his religious and political goals. The following discussions are aimed to shed light on the scientific facts and other knowledge trampled during the attacks on natural science, cosmology, democracy, morality, and Atheism.

Themes

D'Souza starts by inventing "themes" that Atheists follow in their war on Christianity. He does not say who the Atheists are or what Atheist organizations are at war. He lumps all Atheists into a homogeneous group that acts as a single body.

D'S Quote: The distinguishing element of modern atheism is its intellectual militancy and moral self-confidence.

Comment: The first theme is a false assertion of intellectual militancy for all Atheists. Atheists have a strong intellectual position which is based on the validity of natural science theories and on their support of religious freedom—a goal they have been seeking for thousands of years. Some militant Atheists are upset over continuous intrusions by militant Christians into secular natural science and secular democracy and express themselves strongly when that happens, but these militant Atheists are few in number.

Christians have had the option to respect scientific theories. On many occasions, though, they have instead turned to pseudo-scientific religious theories, knowing full well the scientific community would reject them. The use of supernatural theories, after all, does not withstand examination. An example is D'Souza's support for the failed supernatural Intelligent Design pseudo-science theory as a replacement for Darwin's Theory. This subject will be covered in detail later.

D'S Quote: A second major theme of atheist discourse is the historical crimes of religion. The Crusades, the Inquisition, the religious wars, and the witch trials all feature prominently in this moral indictment.

Comment: The second theme, moral indictment for past Christian crimes, has been well earned and recorded by history. The Crusades, the Inquisition, the religious wars, and the witch trials in Europe and America were all activities by Christian churches or theocratic organizations that should be remembered for their crimes and condemned. History has indicted other organizations for comparable moral crimes, and accordingly, Christians should be held to the same standard. Humanity should document and preserve the histories of all major killings.

D'S Quote: *Christianity is the main foundation of Western civilization, the root of our most cherished values.*

Comment: Certainly Christianity has been a major contributor to our Western values, and indeed it should be honored for its many contributions to the West. However, there were earlier contributors to Western civilization including: Greek, Persian, Roman, Egyptian and Anglo-Saxon. However societal laws and values evolve, and many have been added to the cherished values of American democracy through new laws. This includes women's rights, abolition of slavery, homosexual rights, gay marriage, and religious freedom. At times, Christianity has opposed some of the "*most cherished values*" which have emerged from our American democracy.

During the period of Western Enlightenment, the Church was the dominant governing power in the West. When faced with modernity, Christian theocracies many times resisted change and defended their old religious dogma and values, even when detrimental to Western democratic values. The Christian Church's inward and defensive actions impeded the advance of some cherished Western values, personal freedoms, democratic governance, and scientific knowledge. It did so by imposing supernatural religious "truths" that it deemed superior in all cases to natural "truths." Some cherished Western values could be made possible only when Christian theocracies were rejected and replaced by secular democracies, for American democratic values could be only from the authority of the secular populous, the people, and not from a Christian God.

D'S Quote: It is reasonable to have faith.

Comment: Faith is a personal belief and a religious freedom for all Americans. Under American democracy, citizens are able to choose or not choose religions of their choice, for the freedom of religion is fundamental to American democracy. It is therefore reasonable to have faith but equally reasonable to have no faith. This is the opposite of the philosophy of Christian theocracies that demand only one faith. By authorizing only one faith, they make followers of all others Atheists or heretics.

D'S Quote: This is not a religious war, but a war over religion, and it has been declared by leading Western atheists who have commenced hostilities.

Comment: As a minority, Atheists are a small, disorganized group that could not start, much less conduct, a war. They are simply independent souls who defy being herded. Why would they start a war with Christians? Christians have all the advantageous forces. In the United States, the majority of Americans are Christians and believe in the Bible (28 percent believe that it is the actual word of God, 47 percent that it contains inspired words but not actual ones of God, and 21 percent that it is a fable). Atheists are in this last and smallest category.

The war D'Souza is worried about is not a war at all. It can be explained as a normal contest of religious beliefs over secular ideas emerging in society after advances in natural science, democracies, and rational philosophy. If so, why can Christendom not defend its claim to greatness in the open arena of public debate? Does D'Souza advocate that Christians should "win" by giving the government theocratic powers of censorship over natural science, democratic laws, and public education? Should scientists be forced to allow the supernatural into natural science? Should Atheists be limited in their speech in American democracy to keep their evils from the public? A "win" by Christians in this hypothetical war would have a Christian theocracy replace American's secular democracy.

The defense of natural science and secular democracy has been and will continue to be a worthy struggle. D'Souza might wish to call it a war, but whatever the label, it is a worthy struggle by Americans to retain democratic values.

Zacharias's Book

The second book attacking Atheists, *The Real Face of Atheism,* gets praise from Christian Fundamentalists. This includes the religious icon Billy Graham. Graham's support confirms that Ravi Zacharias's views are representative of evangelical ministers.

Zacharias asserts that he will expose the hopelessness of Atheism and reveal God's authority in all things, even in the secular field of science and constitutional democracy. After Sam Harris wrote his book *The End of Faith*, Zacharias felt the need for a Christian reply, and in 2008 he did so with his book *The End of Reason*, which attacks Harris as an

Atheist and labels his book as an Atheist book. We need not critique this book, for his attacks on Atheists only repeats those expressed in his book. Further attacks on Atheists by a militant Fundamentalist will not give us any additional information about supernatural Christian views on Nature, science or secular government so they are not included.

Zacharias makes a false link between Atheists and natural science. Natural science is neither religious nor atheistic. It is just fact-based observations of Nature. Christians and Atheists can do equally good or bad science. The scientific process is important—not the religious beliefs of the experimentalist making the measurements or the theorists writing the equations. The scientific process does not allow the supernatural. Observations of Nature must support the scientific theories.

Apparently, it is difficult for ministers and theologians to accept that religious and biblical "truths" that are useful in Christian supernatural narratives and sermons are not "truths" or facts in the natural scientific world. They cannot accept that Atheists can get "truths" about Nature just fine for without a supernatural God: planets move in their orbits according to the laws of physics, stars shine brightly from the energy of nuclear fusion, and stars explode at the end of their lives for the lack of nuclear fuel and fling star dust into space. From there, the dust coalesces through gravity, forms planets (including Earth), and serves as the material from which all biological life (including humans) emerged.

However, as *Homo sapiens* evolved from primates and struggled to find resources and food for survival, they also began a search to understand the daunting mysteries of life and the beauty of art. In addition to using Nature's truths, humans found that they could invent supernatural stories to provide spiritual guidance and community identity. Now we know the difference it is important to disentangle the two "truths", Nature's and God's, for they are from different sources and serve different needs. Zacharias muddles them, but the following discussion attempts to separate the natural scientific "truths" from supernatural religious "truths."

Approach

Zacharias uses D'Souza's writing approach of leading with false assertions which includes announcing what Atheists and scientists think. Zacharias, however, is neither. He damns Atheists and natural science, including the secular teachings of the scientific community on many subjects; biological evolution, cosmology, and neuroscience. All these scientific subjects are in conflict with his Fundamentalist Christian supernatural beliefs. Considerable similarities exist in the subjects of the attacks on Atheists by D'Souza and Zacharias, but they differ in the details of their arguments. Comments on each quote are addressed separately to capture the detailed arguments each author uses.

3

THE ATTACKS

THE ATTACKS ON Atheists are discussed by subjects the two authors believe have been used by Atheists to harm Christianity. These are the very same subjects of modernity which Christians have resisted changing. These subjects are common in the two books. The attacks by each author are kept separate to retain their point of view.

Atheists—D'Souza

D'Souza begins his attacks on the evils of Atheists by inventing an evil motivation for them.

    D'S Quote: *Atheism is motivated not by reason but by a kind of cowardly moral escapism.*

    <u>Comment</u>: A few pages after asserting that Atheists are motivated by "*a kind of cowardly moral escapism*," D'Souza then accuses Atheists of intellectual militancy. In reality, reason motivates Atheism, and this no more leads to cowardly moral escapism than religion does. D'Souza fails to give examples of cowardly moral escapism committed by Atheists, so this invented evil cannot be addressed further.

Leading a moral life is not the unique product of any one religion or belief system. Human morality has naturally evolved and is found universally in people around the world. Differences can be culturally and religiously based. Morality's sources (Nature or God) and its manifestation by Atheists or Christians are examined later.

D'S Quote: _Atheism, not religion, is responsible for the mass murders of history._

Comment: Both Christians and Atheists have committed mass murders in history. The Christian Bible describes the great biblical flood as a worldwide genocide commanded by God. The theocratic ruler Pope Urban II launched the Christian Crusades in 1096, and this resulted in the recapture of Jerusalem with widespread killing. The Christian moral doctrine for a holy crusade[7] included two assumptions which the Vatican could interpret to meet the situations of the crusades they confronted.

1) _Christ is concerned with the political order of humanity, and he intends for his agents on Earth (kings, popes, bishops, etc.) to establish on Earth a Christian republic that is a single, universal, transcendental state ruled by Christ through the lay and clerical magistrates he endows with authority._

2) _Violence and its consequences (death and injury) are morally neutral rather than intrinsically evil, and whether violence is good or bad is a matter of intention._

These doctrines gave the crusaders free passes to commit mass killing and atrocities against the Muslims in the Holy Land, a war that continued on and off for two hundred years. There were other crusades as well. In Europe in 1209, Pope Innocent III initiated a twenty-year military crusade to eliminate Catharism—a Christian movement the Vatican considered heretical. It was conducted in the south of France with the killing of about a million people.

Mass killings are not limited to the Crusades. Christians just did their share of killing when in power. With theocratic power in governments decreasing in Europe after the Middle Ages, non-theistic powers were the major wagers of wars. Christians on both sides led World War I, which ended up costing about a hundred million lives. World War II killed about the same number, with the non-theist Joseph Stalin killing over twenty millions of his citizens to solidify his ruling power, and Adolph Hitler was responsible for another twenty million deaths.

In short, the lists of mass killings is long for both Christian and non-Christian governments. There is no factual information supporting D'Souza's assignment of blame only to non-theist or atheistic governments.

D'S Quote: _Regular church goer numbers in Europe, depending on the country, [are] between 10 and 25 percent of the population. Only one in five Europeans says that religion is important in life. Czech president Vaclav Havel has rightly described Europe as "the first atheistic civilization in the history of mankind." Still, some 40 percent of Americans say they attend church on Sundays. More than 90 percent of Americans believe in God, and 60 percent say their faith is important to them._

Comment: Many reasons exist for the large increase in secularism and Atheism in Europe and, to a lesser degree, in America. In Europe there is a long history of religious wars, and from that memory there is a strong desire to avoid them. Further, Europe more broadly recognizes the secular Enlightenment's contribution to humanity, secular science and philosophy. Most of these advances have occurred not only without any involvement of the Church but often in opposition to the Church.

D'S Quote: For atheists, the solution is to weaken the power of religion worldwide and to drive religion from the public sphere so that it can no longer influence public policy.

But how should religion be eliminated? Our atheist educators have a short answer: through the power of science.

Atheists do not bother to disbelieve in Baal or Zeus and invoke them only to make all religion sound silly. The atheists' real target is the God of monotheism, usually the Christian God.

Comment: Atheists do not seek _to "weaken the power of religion"_ except when religion steps on science's turf, such as in public school natural science classes where science takes steps to remove supernatural religion. Religious organizations that receive tax benefits should "_no longer influence public policy,_" but individual believers are free to vote however they desire. The aim of the scientific community and the government is not to eliminate religion, only to keep it separated from natural science and the government.

The phrase "_atheist educators_" is false labeling aimed at public educators and science educators in general. The religious belief of an educator should be personal and unimportant. It is only the quality of education and the separation of science from religion that matters. Atheist educators can be as good or bad at their jobs as their Christian counterpoints, but in all cases, the classroom's scientific facts are to be Nature based.

D'Souza forgets that in our constitutional democracy, religion is separate from and cannot be supported by the government. Natural science is a secular subject and teachers in public schools cannot inject supernatural religious material into their classrooms.

A secular education is not "*cultural suicide.*" If a person wants his or her child to be educated in the sciences, it can only be through the secular language of science. Educators, teachers, and professors come from diverse backgrounds and are teaching because they are qualified in their specific secular subjects—physics, chemistry, English, and so on. If they want a Christian religious education, there are religious schools available.

D'Souza gives no data to support his anti-religious assertion against educators but continues to blast educators in public schools.

<u>D'S Quote</u>: *Children spend the majority of their waking hours in school. Parents invest a good portion of their life savings in college education to entrust their offspring to people who are supposed to educate them. Isn't it wonderful that educators have figured out a way to make parents the instruments of their own undoing? Isn't it brilliant that they have persuaded Christian moms and dads to finance the destruction of their own beliefs and values? Who said atheists weren't clever?*

<u>Comment</u>: Parents have choices about what schools or colleges their children attend. Public schools and colleges are secular by law, but there are also religious schools and colleges that parents may select for their children's religious instruction.

Atheists are not factors in the decisions about children's education. Those are the parents' decisions. D'Souza's tale about "*clever atheists*" is just a fairy tale about evil Atheists lurking under each school desk.

D'S Quote: *The atheists' real target is the God of monotheism, usually the Christian God.*

Comment: D'Souza treats Atheists as an organized threat that acts as one against a target. This, of course, has never been the case. They act as citizens who have their own independent thoughts on problems and vote accordingly. Atheists are also less than 20 percent of the population. What is the problem with the Christian majority winning its arguments in a democracy?

"Atheist" and "pagan" are old words religious believers have used to describe others—ones not of their religion. They are a minority and easy targets for Fundamentalists to accuse them for any and all things. The Fundamentalist Jerry Falwell blamed the terrible 9/11 terrorist attack in New York on many people. This included essentially everyone he considered foes of Christendom.

> *The pagans and the abortionists and the feminists and the gays and the lesbians who are actively trying to make that an alternative lifestyle, the ACLU, People for the American Way— all of them who have tried to secularize America. I point the finger in their face and say, "You helped this [9/11] happen."*

D'Souza follows this same pattern as that of Falwell and other Fundamentalist Christians—make false assertions about Atheists targeting the Christian God. Did D'Souza not understand that it was a religious cult (Islamist Al Qaeda) doing harm in order to promote their religious goals?

D'S Quote: The atheists no longer want to be tolerated. They want to monopolize the public square and to expel Christians from it. They want political questions like abortion to be divorced from religious and moral claims. They want to control school curricula so they can promote a secular ideology and undermine Christianity. They want to discredit the factual claims of religion, and they want to convince the rest of society that Christianity is not only mistaken but also evil. They blame religion for the crimes of history and for the ongoing conflicts in the world today. In short, they want to make religion—and especially the Christian religion—disappear from the face of the earth.

Comment: This paragraph is a broadside attack against Atheists in general. Every one of the seven attacks in this paragraph is a false assertion by D'Souza.

The atheists no longer want to be tolerated.

Toleration is something a superior gives an underling. The problem for D'Souza is that all religious minorities, including Atheists, in our American democracy are to be treated equally. The Christian majority does not dispense toleration to underling minorities. It is the country that offers equal citizenship to all—even Atheists. Christians must be reminded this is not a theocracy where one religion can tolerate others but a secular democracy where all religions are treated equally.

Atheists as a group are believers of reason and seek only to have each major discipline (science, government, and religion) be independent and stand on its merits in the public square.

They [Atheists] want to monopolize the public square and to expel Christians from it.

Two false assertions are in this sentence. Atheists do not want to monopolize the public square. In fact, how would they? For they are a minority. They want only equality with the others in the discussions. They also do not want to expel Christians from the public square. In public forums, it is up to each participant to listen or not listen, or to be there or not. Further, Atheists are a minority. How can they expel any larger group—particularly the Christians, who are five times larger in numbers?

> *They [Atheists] want political questions like abortion to be divorced from religious and moral claims.*

First, the right to an abortion is a law (*Roe v. Wade*), not apolitical question. Atheists do not want to control the public discussion on abortion, or any other subject. Abortion is one of many public health questions as well as one of many moral issues discussed in public health. Thus, discussions must include both the health issue and the moral issue, and they must include people of all religious persuasions.

> *They [Atheists] want to control school curricula so they can promote a secular ideology and undermine Christianity.*

In American democracy, the school curricula must be secular. The promotion of any one religion reduces the religious freedom for all others. Christianity is not undermined when treated as any other religion outside of the secular curricula. There is no Christian component to be controlled in natural science discussions in schools. Churches have the option of having their own religious schools where they are free to control the agenda for their Christian students outside of public schools.

Of course the classroom subjects in public schools are secular, for those are the only ones that can be taught. There is no ideology involved; it's only the fact that the courses must be secular. Teaching religious courses with Christian, Muslim, or Hindu ideology would violate the separation of church and state.

They [Atheists] want to discredit the factual claims of religion, and they want to convince the rest of society that Christianity is not only mistaken but also evil.

Factual claims of religion are open for critiques as are the facts presented for all other subjects. It is up to society to decide whether their claims are factual or evil. Atheists and non-believers make up only 20 percent of the population. Christians are in the majority, so Christianity should do well in social discussions of the facts. Calling something "evil" is what religious people do to other people. It is not a term scientists or Atheists use.

They [Atheists] blame religion for the crimes of history and for the ongoing conflicts in the world today.

Atheists hold Christians and non-Christians equally responsible for their past acts. Neither should get a free pass from their past histories. The conflicts are discussed later.

They [Atheists] want to make religion—and especially the Christian religion—disappear from the face of the earth.

Atheists do not have the desire or capability to make any religion or subject disappear from the face of the Earth. This is simply a false assertion with no foundation.

In brief, D'Souza's assertions are factually erroneous but nevertheless are offered as facts to demonize Atheists and scientists and to lead readers to appreciate the greatness of Christendom. D'Souza's sermon on Christendom's war with Atheists is designed to support the Christian supernatural narrative. But in the natural world where we all live the assertions are an attack on people embracing reason and natural science.

Oddly, D'Souza's assertions about religious greatness do not include any discussion of Christian services to humanity. The author leaves this out. He apparently wishes only to fight wars with Atheists while overlooking Christianity's central message of loving one's neighbor—the opposite message to that of going to war. There are real and pressing humanitarian issues to tackle around the world that Christians and Atheists are engaged in. Surely, Christian apologists should focus their energies on solving the pressing problems of humanity instead of fighting wars with perceived evildoers. In the end, D'Souza's failed arguments only render the efforts of Christians to work together with Atheists and other non-Christians much more difficult by leading the discussion into false wars.

Atheists—Zacharias

Zacharias also paints a dim picture of how Atheists are able to see the world. He makes specific statements about what he believes are the evil things they do and think. He assumes (falsely) that all Atheists think and do the same thing, and he assumes (falsely) he has magical insight into their thoughts.

Z Quote: In this study of atheism we have seen the logical contradictions it embraces, the existential hell it creates, and the vacuous pronouncements it makes. This manifold vulnerability is what provoked the acerbic remark that atheism has a greater capacity to smell rotten eggs than to lay good ones, or to attack other systems than to defend its own.[8]

Comment: Zacharias's depth of feeling about Atheism is evident when he uses the image of an "*existential hell*" and his need to address their "*vacuous pronouncements.*" Hell is a Christian term, not one that Atheists use. However, Zacharias knows well that if he stays within the bounds of the supernatural words of God's narrative and references biblical supernatural actions as metaphors, there would be no conflicts with scientists or Atheists. But he knowingly steps into Nature's world and attacks natural science with religious supernatural pseudo-science theories. He also knows full well the scientific community, biotech companies around the world, and all major universities in the United States and Europe will not support injecting the supernatural into natural science. This includes Cambridge University, which he once attended.

Z Quote: Atheism has borne this [moral] offspring, and it is her legitimate child—with no mind to look back to for her origin, no law to turn to for guidance, no meaning to cling to for life, and no hope for the future.

Comment: Zacharias sees Atheists as a sad, no-hope group without a God to provide laws or a place to turn to for guidance and the meaning of life. Actually, Atheists see things far differently. They see Nature, humanity, and reason to turn to for guidance, meaning in life, and have much hope for the future.

Zacharias fails to give specific references to support his attacks. For example, what Atheist has said there is

"*no law to turn to for guidance… and no hope for the future*"?

Carl Sagan and Stephen Hawking are two examples of Atheists who have elegantly described where they get their guidance and meaning to life. They've done so in their books and television programs, which have provided many millions of people with inspiration.

Z Quote: *Atheists must make sense out of a random first cause, denounce as immoral all moral denunciation, express meaningfully all meaninglessness, and find security in hopelessness.*

Comment: Zacharias gives his summary of Atheists with three false assertions.

[They] make sense out of a random first cause.
For Atheists a first cause for the creation of the universe is not a religious or moral problem but a scientific one. Christians might offer their supernatural biblical narrative for creation, and that is fine for believers. A religious belief requires no experimental proof. Atheists, however, look to physicists for answers. They must operate within the natural laws of Nature and present proof.

At this time "*a random first cause*" is described by quantum theory[9] and is a leading explanation of the creation of the universe described by the Big Bang theory. Many experimental and theoretical activities are underway to gather more proof this is how Nature got everything going.

[They] denounce as immoral all moral denunciation.
Atheists and Christians both search for morals to guide their lives. The difference is where they look and the rules they use. Christians believe the words of their God give all the moral guidance they need. Far from denouncing as immoral all Christian morals, Atheists seek a broader base and study morals from secular philosophers as well as theologians. One example is Thomas Jefferson.

Although called an Atheist by many he researched all the works of secular and religious philosophers and theologians from the many books he could get his hands on in order to arrive at his personal guiding moral philosophy.

> *[They] express meaningfully all meaninglessness, and find security in hopelessness.*

Scientists today are happily conducting physics research on the creation of the universe and biological research on the creation of humans without any feelings of meaninglessness or hopelessness. In fact, it's just the opposite. Experimentalists are providing exciting new observations, such as the discovery of a new particle, the Higgs boson—a prediction from the Standard Model of physics. Theorists are happily trying to prove they need more data to complete the model and/or change it. Making sense out of a "*random first cause*" might sound crazy, but physicists attempting to understand Nature find that Nature appears occasionally to do crazy (to the non-scientist) things.

<u>Z Quote</u>: *The atheist, recognizing no law of his own being other than survival, finds himself a constant slave of the moment. One may then walk down a slippery slope into further bondage and self-defacement, finally to become a number, imprisoned by the self-gratifying desires of others.*

<u>Comment</u>: Zacharias again paints a sorry picture of Atheists, but these comments are simply not based on facts. Atheists are not slaves of the moment, they do not walk down slippery slopes, and the desires of others do not imprison them. Further, Atheists recognize the laws of the land as do Christians. Atheists don't recognize the laws of the Christian Church only because they don't

believe. Similarly, Christians don't recognize the laws of the Buddhists or those of any other religion for they believe differently.

D'Souza made a similar attack, and the comment offered in reply noted this was certainly not the case with many of the Founding Fathers who were Atheists or Deists. They did not slip into "*further bondage and self-defacement.*" One does not see this in the Constitution—a product of the Founding Fathers, who were a collection of Atheists, Deists, and Christians. They were certainly not slaves of the moment.

What Atheist does Zacharias know who has said he or she is "*imprisoned by the self-gratifying desires of others*"? Atheists are citizens and no more imprisoned than Christians or adherents of any other religion. They all honor the laws of the Constitution. This is a prime example of a false assertion with no support.

Z Quote: *The atheist, on the other hand, having rejected God, flutters between pleasurable options, with inner peace forever eluding him.*

Comment: Most Atheists have inner peace, and they do not "*flutter between pleasurable options.*" Atheists recognize that people enact the laws of the land. They practice common decency, which can be passed on from parents and/or community. Atheists reject a supernatural God for themselves, but recognize that others might find inner peace from belief in gods, the Christian God or the gods of other religions.

Z Quote: *Atheism walks with its head down, earthbound, which is why it grasps nothing of eternal value. It must admit its predicament: without God, there is no meaning to life.*

Comment: This dramatic and sad picture does not describe Atheists. Atheists have no problems walking with their heads up high, having meaning in their lives, or grasping for the eternal value of Nature.

Thomas Jefferson was labeled an Atheist, but his peers selected him for his grasp of eternal values. The Declaration of Independence he authored is a good example of universal societal values, and with the approval of the Continental Congress and ratification by the states, it conveyed the societal values of America.

Natural Science

Natural science is man's tool for understanding Nature, and its authority comes from the scientific community. Although great progress has been made, there are still many questions about Nature remaining to be answered. It is OK for scientists to say "I don't know the answer." In fact, scientists say that they may not know enough on some subjects to even formulate an intelligent question at this time, and that is also OK. The uncertainty of not having all of the answers allows some Christians to rush in and fill a hole in knowledge by saying God must have done it. This is the case with the incomplete knowledge scientists have about the initial spark causing the Big Bang and the first self-replicating molecule of life. Scientists just keep chipping away at answers to these basic questions, but they also carefully keep a supernatural God out as an answer in their work.

D'Souza declares that natural science is a product of Christendom, but he fails to recognize that science is a universal activity of all peoples of all religions and was practiced thousands of years before the first Christian. And over the years advances in science have occurred in many countries by many people other than Christians.

D'S Quote: Yet science as an organized, sustained enterprise arose only once in human history. And where did it arise? In Europe, in the civilization then called Christendom.

Comment: History has shown that science is a universal activity of all peoples. Individuals in countries throughout the world have advanced scientific knowledge. Some half-million years ago, our ancestors learned how to make fire, and about the same time period, they started to make stone tools. Both of these were major scientific advances.

There were Greek scientists before Christ, and there have been many subsequent scientific contributions by non-Christians. This includes Muslim scientists and mathematicians in the Middle East, as well as scientists of various Eastern regions in India and China.

The scientific revolution in the fifteenth century included earlier work by Muslim scientists restoring older natural knowledge from the Greeks that had been largely lost. In doing so, they made it available to European scientists. Additionally the excellent planetary and stellar observational data Muslims observed between the eighth and thirteenth centuries also made its way to Europe. Copernicus subsequently used this in his formulation of the helio-centric theory of the cosmos. Science prospered in the West from the rise of educational institutions mainly supported by the Church. These institutions increased the opportunities for hopeful scientists to receive an education and work in science.

D'Souza incorrectly puts the Catholic Church as the driving force for the scientific advances. In reality, it was the individual Catholic and

Protestant scientists who made the scientific advances. In many cases, their advances were in spite of the Church bureaucracy which in many cases attempted to stop any advance that did not correspond with its dogma. This applied to the work of Galileo and others.

The largest institutional church was Roman Catholic, and it generally hindered any scientific advance for its highest priority was to defend its dogmas—the source of its power—against any new competitive theories. Protestant churches were not any better. The advancement of natural science and everything else new was a distant second to maintaining the Christian dogma. Science advanced in spite of the Christian church and its dogma—not because of it.

Even today some Fundamentalist's churches deny biological evolution and the Big Bang's physical creation of the universe. Other Christian denominations are trying to move forward, but most are stuck halfway between divine creation of man and the universe and the secular theories of scientists. This was recently illustrated when Pope Francis said,

> *Evolution in nature is not inconsistent with the notion of creation, because evolution requires the creation of beings that evolve.... God should not be seen "as a magician with a magic wand."*

These statements appear to go a step beyond those of the previous popes, including Pope Benedict XVI whose anti-science position put forward the pseudo-science Intelligent Design theory when talking about evolution. The pope's words are contradictory to the biblical narrative for they attempt to link the creation of Adam and Eve (supernatural characters) with evolution (a natural theory) which prohibits the supernatural. Whether any pope will take a real step toward recognizing natural science remains to be seen. The difficulty for a pope to take that step is appreciated, but this pope's position really does not give approval to Darwin's Theory. It attempts to finesse natural science with a wish to not confront it. The scientist Jerry Coyne[10] sums up the pope's position:

> *You'll find that tinges of creationism remain. In fact, the Vatican's official stance on evolution is explicitly unscientific: a combination of modern evolutionary theory and Biblical special creationism. The [Catholic] Church hasn't yet entered the world of modern science.*

It is a small step forward from the awkward position of Pope Benedict, who could not get beyond supporting the discredited Intelligent Design pseudo-science theory. Catholics have a long way to go to match the progress of Progressive Christians who accept natural science without qualifications.

D'S Quote: Science was founded between the thirteenth and fourteenth centuries through a dispute between two kinds of religious dogma. The first kind held that scholastic debate, operating according to the strict principles of deductive reason, was the best way to discover God's hand in the universe. The other held that inductive experience, including the use of experiments to "interrogate nature," was the preferred approach. Science benefited from both methods, using experiments to test propositions and then rigorous criticism and argumentation to establish their significance.

Comment: Science was not founded in the thirteenth and fourteenth centuries. It had been going on long before. For example, the first major scientific advance was making fire about half a million years ago, followed by making stone tools. It took scientific knowledge to make fire and stone, copper, bronze and later iron tools. Early Greeks, such as Archimedes in the third century BC, did science. So did the Egyptians and Persians. It merely became more organized with procedures and processes by Catholic and Protestant scientists a thousand years later.

Where was the deductive reasoning to place God's hand in the universe when the Vatican supported the failed Ptolemaic geocentric theory and attacked Galileo for supporting the correct heliocentric theory? The answer is that the Church was defending its dogma and not following deductive reasoning or any science procedure. Priests and friars made many scientific advances, but many times the Church was a drag on the development of new science.

Most early scientists were Christian, and many saw themselves as achieving God's purpose by going beyond God's biblical words and exploring the universe. These scientists were careful to collect data as observed without injecting God. Copernicus later used the secular experimental data in his formulation of the heliocentric theory, and Kepler used it for his theories on planetary orbits as well. These theories did not include God.

In 1620 Francis Bacon was instrumental in laying the foundations for the modern scientific methodology. Newton's theory of planetary motion and gravity in 1687 worked in the cosmos and on the Earth. The new theories did not employ divinity to explain planetary motion in the heavens or falling objects on Earth. The same secular theory described both. In Franklin's experiments in the clouds and on the Earth in 1752, he demonstrated that lightning, once viewed as a sign from God in the heavens, was a natural electrical discharge that could be readily demonstrated here on Earth.

D'Souza attempts to paint scientists as restricting natural science so that miracles and the supernatural are excluded. They are indeed excluded, but D'Souza fails to understand why. Science works by requiring experimental verification of theories about Nature, and Nature does not include the supernatural. Science says only that it has the best theories to explain the data available from Nature. When the data changes, the theories must agree or be changed.

D'Souza accuses science of being "hung up" on its dogma of no supernatural occurrences, such as God not being the supernatural designer in evolution. Of course science is "hung up." There would be no natural science if there were a supernatural God involved.

D'S Quote: There is nothing in science that makes miracles impossible.

Comment: There is nothing in natural science that makes miracles impossible or possible. Science simply does not address miracles, and supernatural miracles cannot coexist with natural science. Miracles have a home only in supernatural religious narratives and other human-made stories. Such stories are useful literary devices for enhancing the power of advertising a supernatural, leaders, their actions in supernatural places like heaven and hell.

Not respecting that the scientific process excludes the supernatural, Zacharias attacks Atheists for not believing in miracles.

Z Quote: *The atheist's prejudice against miracles robs him of the miraculous nature of the world itself.*

Comment: Atheists and scientists indeed reject miracles, and it is not a prejudice but a commandment by the scientific community to not employ the supernatural. Nature's grandeur is there for anyone (including Atheists) to see, ponder, and appreciate. Indeed, many books by Atheists attest to the wonders of Nature, such as Carl Sagan's popular book *Cosmos*. If Zacharias had talked to Atheists, he would have found they do not feel robbed. Nature's wonders, after all, speak for themselves.

D'S Quote: *Modern science was designed to exclude a designer....It doesn't matter how strong or reliable the evidence [for a supernatural designer] is; scientists, acting in their professional capacity, are obliged to ignore it.*

Comment: Modern science was and is being designed by the secular scientific community. Modern science excludes a supernatural biological designer simply because Nature designs without a designer. D'Souza wants to have God as the supernatural designer and cannot accept there is no evidence for a supernatural one. In fact, it is just the opposite. All experimental evidence supports that Nature designs the physical universe and biological life without a designer. The rainbow is a simple example. A beautiful rainbow in the sky is the result of sunlight striking raindrops that act as prisms and refract the white light into its components of the electromagnetic spectrum. The short wavelengths are violet, the longer ones are red, and the other wavelengths are in between. No designer or God is required for a bueatiful rainbow.

Zacharias attacks Atheists by asserting that their views prevent scientists from doing their jobs around the world. First he asserts (falsely) that biological evolution violates the laws of physics.

Z Quote: The ascending of biological forms into more complex and superior designs also comes into conflict with the Second Law of Thermodynamics in Physics. Thermodynamics is that branch of physical science that is concerned with the interrelationship and interconversion of different forms of energy, and the behavior of systems as they relate to certain basic quantities such as pressure and temperature.

Comment: This is simply an incorrect statement. The second law of thermodynamics is honored in all natural science, and that includes biological evolution described by Darwin's Theory. Somebody slipped Zacharias misleading physics information after he left Cambridge.

Z Quote: Atheism actually does more to destroy science than theology. Huxley would have done better to have concentrated on the internecine warfare within the scientific world itself, where scientific theories and beliefs have fallen by the wayside as new finds decimate old ones. The move from Ptolemy to Copernicus to Newton to Einstein, and to the high value placed on Quantum Theory, has massive leaps within it.

Comment: Julian Huxley's comments were made 150 years ago and centered on Darwin's Theory of natural selection. This theory has not destroyed science, and as Cambridge University notes, Darwin's Theory has proven necessary to understanding biological evolution. (See appendix A, Cambridge Biology Course–Evolution and Behaviour.)

Science merely wants to get theology off its turf and to let natural science speak for itself. If a scientific theory works without God, then so be it. That is how Nature works. Science does not ask whether the scientists are Atheistic or religious. It only requires scientists to do good science. Darwin started his career as a Christian, but over the years he lost his belief. His science was unaffected during this time of transition in his religious life. He carefully separated natural science from the supernatural Christian religion. He was also careful to support his wife's Christianity, which she retained throughout her life with him.

Internecine warfare is normal in science or any competitive discipline. It is a source of strength, for scientific theories are always up for questioning. New theories must fight for existence by providing evidence to replace older, incorrect, entrenched ones. This is how Nobel Prizes are generally awarded. They are given to the winners of these scientific battles. Einstein's theory of general relativity included time and replaced Newton's theory of gravity which did not. Both men, however, are still honored for their contributions. Obviously, Zacharias does not understand that internecine warfare in the scientific community is not only common but a good, productive thing.

Finally, religious belief embracing Christian or any supernatural theology cannot destroy natural science. Science is based on observations of Nature, and that is independent of any words attributed to a supernatural God.

Z Quote: *In the end, the atheistic view reduces the botanist from studying daffodils to fertilizing them, the scientist from measuring the "big bang" to becoming a small fizzle, and the geologist from investigating the geological column to becoming embedded in one of its layers.*

Comment: Not one example supports this sweeping overview of scientists. Who are these botanists he mentions? There are very few Atheist botanists, scientists, or geologists who would agree with this characterization. An example is Stephen Hawking—an Atheist scientist studying the Big Bang. His theoretical research in cosmology has received international awards, and his books on cosmology for the public have received widespread acclaim. His work has been a big deal in the scientific world—not a "*small fizzle.*"

In the end, Zacharias simply refuses to honor scientists (many of whom are Atheists) or to give authority to natural scientific advances. In essence, he has opted out of accepting the vast amount of knowledge generated from scientific advances for the last five hundred years.

Atheist and non-Atheist botanists, scientists, and geologists use their knowledge to help humankind, and Zacharias has chosen to refuse to watch the progress. One can only hope young Christians see beyond Zacharias's attacks on science and realize they can be both a Christian and a botanist, cosmologist, or geologist. They can engage in science in the natural world and separately embrace Christianity in its supernatural narrative independent of science.

Darwin's Theory

The most indigestible natural science theory for D'Souza, Zacharias, Fundamentalist Christians, and most Moderate Christians is Darwin's Theory of natural selection. Biological evolution addresses the Christian God's central and greatest creation (humans) with a godless theory. Many years of observation and testing have shown that Darwin's Theory is more than a just a theory. It is the foundational theory for understanding all biological life. It has been so technically successful and proven so many times in natural and laboratory observations around the world that it is considered an observable fact. It can no longer be dismissed— although there are still some (including D'Souza and Zacharias) who doggedly continue to do so.

Evolution by natural selection can be seen in the many fossils discovered and the DNA of dead and living life forms. Neil Shubin in his book, *Your Inner Fish,* has provided insights into the evolution of our body from our ancestors over the last 450 million years: fishes to reptiles to mammals to primates to hominins and on to us, Homo sapiens. Examples of our ancestors in the tree of life are many; the basic three-region structure of our brain can be found in sharks, our skin structure from reptiles, our three-bone inner ear used for hearing from mammals, our body structure for bipedal walking from primates and the beginning of our large brain from hominins. There are other body parts we don't use that are still with us, such as our little tail bone from our monkey ancestors. We are basically made up of redesigned and repurposed body parts from our past ancestors.

Science describes a common ancestor of all life on Earth 3.5 billion years ago from which evolution continues today. In a summary of recent progress in paleontology, Michael Novacek[11] noted,

> *Since 2000, we have identified five early hominins, our close prehistoric relatives. And if you think that the fossil record deals only with such changes in million-year scales, think again. Just 50,000 years ago—a blink of an eye in the deep time of paleontology—there were at least three, and maybe four, species of the human lineages cohabiting on this planet. Yet within that span of time, only our own species [Homo sapiens] made it through the evolutionary sieve.*

Such advances in paleontology underlining the role of chance in the evolution of humans are not acceptable to

Fundamentalists. Despite the overwhelming data supporting Darwin's Theory of natural selection, Christians continue to put forward a number of pseudo-science theories supporting the biblical creation story of Adam and Eve and God's involvement as creator and designer of life.

There is a spectrum of Christian acceptance of Darwin's Theory. Fundamentalists don't accept it at all, while Progressive Christians accept the whole theory. Other groups, including the Catholic Church, attempt to appease the scientific community by saying they have no quarrel with Darwin's Theory while in practice, however, they refuse to accept the theory in its fullness when applied to human evolution. Darwinian evolution precludes Adam and Eve[12] appearing as fully formed humans without millions of ancestors pairs in just the hominins branch of the evolutionary tree preceding them. Without an Adam and Eve, there is no Original Sin. What we do have in evolutionary biology the individual, familial, tribal, and group social morals that evolved steadily over many generations from the survival and social pressures on our hominins ancestors for the last six million years. These survival morals included many things called sins today—stealing and killing within one's family and tribe. Christianmoral rules have only been available to our human ancestors from the beginning of Christianity only two thousand years ago.

D'Souza leans toward Fundamentalism. He holds to the belief that a supernatural God created and designed Adam and Eve, and Darwin's Theory is only an inconvenient fact that forces D'Souza to search for arguments to put a Christian spin on evolution. He supports the Intelligent Design pseudo-science theory in order to have a Christian theory of human creation that will allow him to reject Darwin's Theory. His attempts at marrying supernatural religion with human evolution fail because the supernatural creation theory he offers has no experimental support. As the federal judge said on the Christian Intelligent Design theory case, it is not science, it is a religious story.

Zacharias steadfastly refuses to accept the overwhelming evidence supporting Darwin's Theory and seems content confronting the scientific community with religious pseudo-science theories that fail the test of science. The position will not bring him much comfort outside of his religious community.

Z Quote: The conclusion should be clear in our minds. Whether it is Crick's speculation that life could have been shuttled here by a guided missile in bacteria form from another planet, or Monod's exaggeration on chance, Huxley's contention that science has delivered a mortal blow to theology is a pipedream. One of the tragic lessons of this century is that experts within certain fields draw upon their knowledge to prove virtually anything they want to prove, all along ignoring a unifying truth that gives fair recognition to other disciplines. It appears that the real problem lies in the fact that Huxley in his contention, and those who live under its fallout, seeing the micro-processes of the trees, have lost sight of the macro-necessities contained in the forest.

Comment: French biochemist Jacques Monod did not exaggerate the role of chance in natural selection; he just gave his opinions supporting the involvement of chance without apology. Further biological research has demonstrated that absolutely free, blind, pure chance is at the very root of the edifice of evolution.

Science has proven that Darwin's and Monod's views of natural selection correspond to what is found in Nature. Chance is embedded in the natural selection process. Scientists have found that chance is embedded in other natural science theories also, such as quantum mechanics. It might be uncomfortable having chance play such an important role in natural science, but it is just the way Nature works. The certitude in life that Zacharias seeks is found only in the supernatural biblical texts and in the minds of believers.

Z Quote: *The logic of chance origins has driven our society into rewriting the rules, so that utility has replaced duty, self-expression has unseated authority, and being good has become feeling good. These new rules plunge the moral philosopher into a veritable vortex of relativizing.*

<u>Comment</u>: Zacharias has made the mistake of using a scientific theory on one subject to provide new social rules for society, an altogether different subject. Darwin's Theory embraces chance as part of natural selection, and this is just a biological fact.

The moral philosopher is not plunged anywhere but uses the observations of the evolution of morality in human ancestors to forge philosophical insights on morality. Some moral traits are based on inherited morality, and religion and other experiences can modify them.

Z Quote: *One of the key struggles here is in having to deal with the problem of determinism; that is, are we the product of blind chance? Although several philosophers have dealt with this question, up to this point none has been able to present a unifying theory that gives a satisfactory answer.*

<u>Comment</u>: There is no struggle in the scientific community dealing with uncertainty in evolutionary biology. Some theologians and philosophers might struggle with determinism, but the biologist can refer to data to answer the question of how blind chance operates in natural selection.

Chance is involved not only in evolutionary biology. Chance is embedded in the theories of quantum mechanics. In fact, without chance in quantum mechanics, many calculations explaining how Nature works would fail. Atoms that undergo radioactive decay do so by chance described by quantum mechanics theories.

Z Quote: Francis Crick, whose discovery of the DNA molecule has had such a profound effect on genetics and biological life as we know it, has said, "The ultimate aim of the modern movement in biology is in fact to explain all biology in terms of physics and chemistry." Yet, as we progress, we come to a dead end. Biologists have shown that the discovery of the physical basis for the genetic code has made the answer to the question of origins even more elusive. Even if we were to grant that the genetic code is the result of natural selection, it still needs the "machinery" to translate the code into function, and this translation itself depends upon components that are themselves the products of translation. The possibility of this occurring is so small as to amount to zero probability.

Comment: Rather than biologists meeting dead ends or having zero chance of explaining the evolutionary steps, the opposite is being observed in the laboratory. Understanding the change in DNA from living bodies has provided— even for complicated biological systems such as the eye, the blood-clotting system, and others— a digital road map of evolution at the molecular level. In fact, the evolution of a complex system has been documented protein by protein. Perhaps Zacharias should read *The Evolution of Vertebrate Blood Clotting* by Professor Doolittle. (See appendix B, Notes on the Evolution of the Human Eye and Blood-Clotting System.) This describes the step-by-step evolution of the many proteins and sequenced processes required to make blood clotting work for humans and many ancestral species over the last four hundred million years.

Intelligent Design

D'Souza and Zacharias cannot resist their imperative to reject Darwin's Theory and inject God as the supernatural designer behind the Intelligent Design pseudo-science theory as a replacement for Darwin's Theory.

D'S Quote: Darwin's theory of evolution, far from undermining the evidence for supernatural design, actually strengthens it.

Comment: D'Souza is way off base here. He claims natural science supports the supernatural when the actual truth is the opposite. Science rejects the supernatural. Darwin's Theory employs the natural selection process, which embraces species variability and uncertainty and designs without a designer. Having Nature as the authority and designer of evolution precludes, not strengthens, the use of supernatural design.

D'Souza's supernatural Intelligent Design argument is based on the failed supernatural argument of biological design by God that Reverend Paley[13] made two hundred years ago.

D'S Quote: The atheists (Dawkins, et al) have led people away from the real explanation of evolution put forth by the Christian Rev Paley two hundred years ago.

Comment: D'Souza uses Paley's theory over and over even though it has long been rejected. Biological life is clearly not the product of intention and creative design by the Christian God. It is as described in Darwin's Theory of natural selection, which has no intention and no designer. It's incredible that D'Souza (and other Christians) have missed one of humankind's greatest intellectual achievements—the Darwinian Revolution.

People have been led away from Paley's explanation for the creation of humans and drawn to Darwin's Theory simply because it works and Paley's doesn't. The biology departments of all major universities teach Darwin's Theory—not Paley's. That includes Paley's alma mater, Cambridge University, in England.

Z Quote: Take, for example, Michael Behe, who in his book Darwin's Black Box, shows us the irreducible complexity of the human cell, which biological evolution cannot explain. Darwin argued that a human eye evolved from a simpler one, and yet he set aside the essential question of its origin. Behe not only observes Darwin's avoidance of this question but tackles it by describing the chemical changes that are set in motion to generate sight. From the moment a photon hits the retina to the end result of an imbalance of charge that causes a current to be transmitted down the optic nerve to the brain, resulting in sight, a series of chemical reactions have taken place that in evolution's mechanism would have been impossible. Thus Behe concludes that the irreducible complexity of the human cell reveals that biochemically macroevolution is impossible and Darwinism false.

Comment: Zacharias needs to update his understanding of the evolution of a human cell and other human systems, such as the eye. Opposite to what Behe says, there appears to be no irreducible complexity in human cells that biological evolution cannot explain.[14] Many, but not all, complex human systems, such as the eye and blood-clotting system, have been explained. Research on all human systems is not yet complete, but no roadblocks have yet prevented the completion of an understanding all complex human systems. Further, the advances in science's ability to read and understand DNA have greatly boosted the ability of scientists to study the evolution of biological systems.

Michael Behe's attempted replacement of Darwin's Theory with the Intelligent Design pseudo-science theory has long since been refuted by the scientific community. In 2005 a federal court heard the case against the use of Intelligent Design as a science to be taught in public schools. The trial (*Kitzmiller v. Dover*) centered on a school district in Dover, Pennsylvania. The outcome was that the federal judge declared Intelligent Design was only a religious pseudo-science theory and not a science theory; therefore, it was not suitable for science classes in public schools.

Zacharias's reference to Behe on the irreducible complexity of biological systems is simply biologically incorrect. Science has explained the evolution of the human cell, the eye, the blood-clotting system, the lungs, and many other complex parts of the body. See appendix B, Notes on the Biological Evolution of the Human Eye and Vertebrate Blood Clotting, for more details.

Z Quote: Sir Fred Hoyle has argued in his book, The Intelligent Universe, that the idea that life originated by the random shuffling of molecules is "as ridiculous and improbable as the proposition that a tornado blowing through a junkyard may assemble a Boeing 747."

Comment: Hoyle's comments are seventy-five years old and simply have been proven incorrect in the application of chance to biological systems. Others have also used the 747 airplane assembly argument, and this includes Michael Behe with the Intelligent Design theory. As mentioned earlier, however, the scientific community and legal courts rejected the theory of Intelligent Design.

Zacharias needs to update his understanding of evolutionary biology and the difference in the design and construction of a 747 airplane and that of DNA-constructed proteins. The 747 is constructed from a human design over a few years. Its design took ten years. DNA molecules construct human proteins in minutes. Cell design is the result of the natural selection process operating through millions of ancestors over billions of years. The DNA design is without a designer but the natural selection process. The simple comparison of the two is erroneous.

D'S Quote: In summary Christians should be suing to get atheist interpretations of Darwin out. Through evolution, rightly understood, Christians can affirm that the book of nature and the book of scripture are in no way contradictory. In fact, both affirm the notion of a universe and its creatures that are the product of supernatural design and divine creation.

Comment: There is no such thing as an Atheist interpretation of Darwin's Theory. There is only the scientific interpretation. Who makes or uses the theory has no bearing on whether the science is right or wrong. The science must stand on its own regardless of the religious belief of the scientist. D'Souza's statement only affirms his misunderstanding of what Darwin and most scientists actually say—namely, that biological design of all life is without a designer and therefore without the need of divine intervention by any God. Nature's process is the designer of the universe and biological life. Darwin's Theory works in the natural world. It is not an Atheistic theory. It is a scientific theory, and like all other natural science theories, it does not require a supernatural God.

The support of Darwin's Theory of natural selection as the driver in evolutionary biology is universal among major universities and has been summarized quite well by a statement from the Cambridge University biology department: *"Nothing in biology makes sense except in light of [Darwinian] evolution."*

Darwinism

Knowing that Darwin's Theory cannot be dismissed, D'Souza devised a rationale that shifts the dismissal of Darwin's Theory to Darwinism, which is something altogether different. He claims that true Christians understand Darwin's Theory but Atheists do not because Atheists argue for Darwinism. Here are three examples of his attempt to switch Darwin's Theory to Darwinism. They are effectively the old bait-and-switch technique of argument.

D'S Quote: But the universe that lawfully produces finches, moths, and humans is quite clearly the product of intention and creative design. So Dawkins's "refutation" of Paley fails gloriously and completely. Paley was right all along. It should be clear from all this that the problem is not with evolution. The problem is with Darwinism. Evolution is a scientific theory; Darwinism is a metaphysical stance and a political ideology.

D'S Quote: Darwinism is the atheist spin imposed on the theory of evolution.... atheists [are the ones who] convert Darwin's Theory to Darwinism.

D'S Quote: For the defenders of Darwinism, no less than for its critics, religion is the issue. Just as some people oppose the theory of evolution because they believe it to be anti-religious; many others support it for the very same reason. This is why we have Darwinism but not

Keplerism; we encounter Darwinists but no one describes himself as an Einsteinian. Darwinism has become an ideology.

Comment: D'Souza never tires of repeating the falsehood of Paley being right with the Intelligent Design pseudo-science theory and Darwin wrong with his theory of natural selection. The scientific community sees otherwise. Cambridge University (alma mater to both Paley and Darwin) clearly states it supports Darwin's Theory of evolution. One must continue to call attention to D'Souza's mistake of using Paley's theory of Intelligent Design when it appears.

D'Souza attempts to switch a scientific theory (Darwin's Theory) with an ideology (Darwinism) and blame independent parties (Atheists). Scientists and Atheists have no trouble working with Darwin's Theory. However, Darwinism is something totally different. It is an ideological interpretation of Darwin's Theory that can be misapplied to social or political applications. It is separate and independent from Darwin's Theory. D'Souza's lack of an understanding of Darwin's Theory of natural selection leads him to misapply Darwinism to metaphysical and/or political arenas.

Zacharias attempts to confuse the reader by falsely linking social theory, such as that of Karl Marx, with biological evolution described by Darwin's Theory under the title of Darwinism.

Z Quote: For Marx himself, religion was the opiate of the people, the sign of the oppressed, and the only illusory sun that revolved around man, so long as man did not revolve around himself. His rationale behind that dedicatory consideration was that he saw how the Darwinian hypothesis provided the scientific substructure to support his economic infrastructure, on which he could build his man-made utopian superstructure.

Comment: Darwin's Theory is a biology theory. Marx was a social and economics philosopher who dealt with social theories. Whether or not Marx's social theory is correct is left to arguments and tests by social philosophers. Darwin's Theory stands on its own outside of social studies by Marx and others. What social philosophers might offer as social or economic theories employing social Darwinism does not impact the biology theory.

Others who champion Intelligent Design, including Ben Stein, have used Darwinism in a negative manner. John Rennie of *Scientific American* said,

The term is a curious throwback, because in modern biology almost no one relies solely on Darwin's original ideas.... Yet the choice of terminology isn't random: Ben Stein wants you to stop thinking of evolution as an actual science supported by verifiable facts and logical arguments and to start thinking of it as a dogmatic, atheistic ideology akin to Marxism.

4

MORALITY

BOTH D'SOUZA AND Zacharias attempt to make the case that there can be no human morality without their Christian God. However, they first acknowledge that others see a universal morality without God, but then quickly dismisses it.

> _D'S Quote: We find Sam Harris insisting that it is quite possible to develop morality independent of the Christian religion or religion in general. We read Theodore Schick Jr. in Free Inquiry insisting that philosophers as different as John Stuart Mill and John Rawls have demonstrated that it is possible to have a universal morality without God._
>
> _There is a profound confusion here. We get a hint of this when we realize that the term "secular" is itself a Christian term._

Comment: D'Souza indicates that philosophers think it is possible to have universal morality without the Christian God, but he then dismisses this by asserting that

> _secularism is itself an invention of Christianity.... Secular values too are the product of Christianity, even if they have been severed from their original source._

Declaring secular values and philosophy as *"an invention of Christianity"* is a stretch even for D'Souza. There were, after all, secular philosophies long before Christianity. In fact, there were secular philosophers long before Christianity appeared, including Epicurus in the third century BC, as previously noted. D'Souza's untruth is another example of his use of the false assertion.

D'S Quote: So man must pay the wages of sin, and the wages of sin is death. This is the second premise of Christianity. The Bible equates death in the biological realm with sin in the moral realm.

So how can a salvation be reconciled with divine holiness and justice? This is posing the question in the right way. The Christian answer is that God decided to pay the price himself for human sin. Not just this sin or that sin but all sin. God did this by becoming man and dying on the cross.

Comment: Sin in the eyes of Christians occurs when one breaks God's laws. Original Sin is a Christian concept described in the supernatural biblical story of the Garden of Eden with Adam, Eve, and a talking serpent. Adam violated God's law forbidding the eating of the fruit from the tree of knowledge. Some denominations say Adam's sin from this act is passed forever afterward to every person. This makes everyone sinful from birth.

D'Souza gives the standard biblical Christian answer for sin in the world: *"God decided to pay the price himself for human sin…by becoming man and dying on the cross."* This moral story is fine for the Christian community but not an acceptable answer to Atheists or believers of other religions. From this initial sinful act by man, Christian morality has had a long and varied history over the years.

Examples of obedience to Christian moral rules over time reveal actions not universally accepted as moral today.

3000 BC (biblical time)—Humanity was judged not to be obedient to God's, commandments and God punished them by killing the human and animal populations in the world, excepting Noah, his family, and selected animals, with a worldwide flood. If taken metaphorically as a biblical supernatural story it causes no conflicts. If taken literally it conflicts with science that cannot support a world-wide flood about 3000 BC.

AD 424—Pagans, pagan libraries and centers of learning in Alexandria and other cities were ruled sinful by the Church and destroyed.

AD 1600—An intellectual (Giordano Bruno) was declared a sinful heretic for expressing views contrary to Church dogma and burned at the stake.

AD 2000—A medical doctor who had performed legal medical services (abortion) was declared a sinful person by the Church and killed by a believer.

The Catholic Church redefined its moral dogma in the mid-1800s and introduced the doctrine of papal infallibility at the First Vatican Council, in 1870. This defined a doctrine concerning faith or morals to be held by the whole Church. At that time the Church's dogma on social moral sins condemned homosexuality, divorce, gay marriage, and non-marital sexual relationships. Because of the power of Christian theocracies, Christian morality was essentially the West's morality for hundreds of years. However, a philosophical shift from old Christian morality to contemporary morality has been underway from the time of the Enlightenment. As the philosopher Gary Gutting[15] noted,

> *In the 17th century most philosophers were religious believers, whereas today most seem to be atheists.*

The philosophical base for what is sinful has changed, and societal laws in many Western countries have removed the accusation of sin from many of the past social dogmas of homosexuality, divorce, marriage, and non-marital sexual relationships. The changes have come from the people voting for new laws. Many Christian churches are struggling to accept these changes.

A majority of contemporary philosophers, Atheists, and many others see that the source of morality is given not by a God on high but by the people. In a secular democracy, citizens of many different religious faiths and no faith work together to establish common secular laws that are agreeable to a majority of citizens. Therefore, the laws cannot be expected to totally conform to those of any one religion, and that includes the Christian moral code.

Atheists say the base of their morals is a result of evolution and subsequent social interactions and education. Natural evolution says there were millions of Adams and Eves—a pair at every branch of the human evolutionary tree. The *Homo sapiens* pair (modern man and woman) appeared about two hundred thousand years ago. Since there was no Christian God, there were no divine laws to break. Therefore, there could not have been any Original Sin. Instead each generation of human ancestors evolved social morals and other survival skills. Personal, familial, tribal, and social morality was a necessary factor in survival. Without cohesion of the social groups, mammalian survival could not have happened.

During the long evolutionary period for mammals, the brain evolved through several stages—a concept[16] neuroscientist Paul MacLean originally formulated in his model in the 1960s. This theory describes a triune brain consisting of three layers: the reptilian complex, the paleomammalian complex (limbic system), and the neomammalian complex (neocortex). Each complex expanded and added new capabilities to the brain through integration with the other complexes. Survivability depended to a degree on the social morality evolved in each subsequent species by natural selection. The integrated multilayered *Homo sapiens* brain of today includes those inherited social morals.

By not accepting the science of moral evolution, D'Souza believes leading scientists and Atheists are destroying belief in an external source of morality—morals from the Christian God. He believes humans will be left with no morality. However, the present generation does have morals. It just happens that many do not accept all the two-thousand-year-old Christian definition of morals and instead have move on to new ones.

D'S Quote: Modern science has, in Pinker's view, destroyed that belief. "The mind is the physiological activity of the brain" and "the brain, like other organs, is shaped by the genes" and those have been "shaped by natural selection and other evolutionary processes." Therefore the mind is nothing more than "an entity in the physical world, part of a causal chain of physical events.

*D'S Quote: If religion...can be systematically ana-
lyzed and explained as a product of the brain's evolution,
its power as an external source of morality will be gone
forever.*

Comment: D'Souza has not accepted the results
of neuroscience research.[17] Pinker rightfully references this regarding the brain's evolution through
natural selection. Atheists would argue there has
never been an *"external source of morality."* However,
Christians are free to believe in this as part of their
supernatural narrative.

Scientists now propose there is also a different
"source of morality" for people to consider. Human
morality appears to be inherited, but many factors can mold it after birth. This includes external
sources such as religious instructions.

In the natural world, morals are products of
Nature's social processes among humans. They are
designed without a designer; they are products of
human evolution. Whether other hominins have
morals is yet to be determined. When humans make
moral mistakes through trial and error, they can
change. Thus, over time humankind's broad range
of moral experience can be enhanced. This process
offers an advantage over gifts of morals from God
that humans cannot correct. After all, who can tell
God to update his morals? This has been painfully
obvious with many of the biblical social morals that
reflect the moral norm of two thousand years ago.
This includes issues of homosexuality, gay marriage,
and premarital sex that have come into conflict with
cultural changes over time.

The recognition of human social interactions
as a source of morals does not negate the importance of Christians' belief in God's proclaimed

morals. This gives Christians and additional set of morals for their use.

In short, scientists argue that humans possess evolved brains with broad mental capabilities and an inherited morality.[18] Humans also have mental capabilities that include the invention of moral storytelling, including epic moral narratives that have supernatural gods.

With a thousand religions offering differing *"external [sources] of morality,"* each will continue to be a source of moral instruction for believers. Studying both the brain's evolution of morals and religion's subsequent contribution to human morals is important to the understanding of human morality.

D'Souza's attacks on morality center on how Atheists use modern science and public education to destroy Christian belief and morality. Zacharias's attacks are aimed more at the lack of moral philosophy of Atheists who do not reference the Christian God to explain moral behavior. Atheist philosophers in the past included the Greek Epicurus, the Roman Lucretius, the Enlightenment-era philosopher Spinoza, and others. For example, Lucretius said,

> *There is no heaven but the one we project on the stars overhead. There is no hell but what our imagination can conjure out of our fears of this world. And there is nothing at all outside of experience that can bring us any more happiness, misery, good, or evil than we can find within the limits of the world we inhabit.*

This obviously differs from the Christian philosophy, but instead of recognizing differences with Atheistic philosophy, Zacharias attacks the Atheist.

In a country with multiple religions, there should be room for other beliefs that bring happiness to the believers.

Z Quote: The atheist has convinced himself that private practices and public behavior are so morally unrelated that the individual can easily draw lines and cross borders without any dirt sticking to one's feet.

Z Quote: The atheist makes two very serious mistakes in his starting point for moral discussion: first, what morality is, and second, what purpose morality serves. He asserts that he can, by the power of unaided reason, arrive at the nature of morality and at a satisfactory moral law.

Comment: These assertions are simply false. They reflect the orthodox Christian view—namely, there is no morality without their God. As noted, many philosophers see morality differently. For example, philosopher Immanuel Kant in his *Groundwork of the Metaphysic of Morals* argues that a person without a direct encounter with Christ and independent of Christ's influence is able to reason and reach the right conclusions on morality.

Many Founding Fathers were Atheists, Deists, or Unitarians, but the majority was Christian. Although they differed in the sources of their morals, they were able by reason to come to mutually acceptable moral judgments on governance. One Founding Father, Thomas Jefferson, was called an Atheist, yet he was the man the Continental Congress chose to write the Declaration of Independence—the document that established the moral basis for the new country declaring independence.

Fundamentalists like D'Souza and Zacharias make a most serious mistake when they attempt to tear down the morals of others. Each religion can argue for the superiority of its moral philosophy, and this presents no conflicts if retained within its religious community, as the Constitution allows. The mistake is when one religion attempts to impose its beliefs on others and on the secular government.

Z Quote: *The atheist starts from social ethics and is never able to anchor morality or its purpose. That starting point is in complete contradiction to the biblical understanding because when man is spiritually dislodged, his reason is estranged from the source of light and he is led into a delirium of vanity.*

Comment: An Atheist is spiritually dislodged from Christian supernaturally gifted morals, but that does not mean all his or her morals are necessarily different. For example, Atheists and Christians can both embrace "Thou shall not kill," "Thou shall not steal," and the Golden Rule— universal moral rules used by many faiths and belief systems. Many of these universal morals were being used centuries before Christianity came into being.

Atheists start by considering human morality described by philosophers from Epicurus to many others to find their source of moral light. A starting point for some Atheists is Immanuel Kant's view on morality:

Morality comes from acts from good will in accordance with moral laws one gives himself, not from external laws from either Nature or God.

Thomas Jefferson anchored his morality in the distillation of the works of many philosophers and religious leaders. This included Jesus, whom he studied from the Bible. Jefferson's library contained 150 books on moral philosophy, and this gave him a broad range of views on morality. One of these books he personally assembled from selected biblical writings from the Christian Gospels to capture the morals of Jesus. It has become known as *The Jefferson Bible.*

Differences in moral philosophy do not dislodge the reason of Atheists from the "*source of light.*" Atheists seek to formulate their own philosophy. Further, an Atheist is not led into a "*delirium of vanity*" nor "*spiritually dislodged.*" An Atheist is not "*spiritually dislodged*" from Christianity, because his or her spiritual foundation is from studying Nature.

Z Quote: Secular philosophers cannot logically give an answer to this question of how to determine right and wrong because there is no common starting point for ethical theorists, and it is not for the lack of trying. Valiant attempts have been made, with some success.

Comment: Secular philosophers, such as Epicurus, Lucretius, Spinoza, and Kant and many philosophers today, give logical arguments on determining right and wrong, and none require a supernatural God. In 1640 the philosopher Bernard Spinoza's book *Tractatus Theologico-Politicus* raised the view that the supernatural scriptures are a work of human literature. He argued that if reason is made subservient to supernatural scriptures,

> *the prejudices of a common people of long ago… will gain a hold on his understanding and darken it.*

Further, as a rationalist philosopher, Spinoza stated,

> *God exists only philosophically.*

It was shocking at that time, and to some people it is still shocking. However, Spinoza is just one of many rational philosophers who have come to grips with the fact that all morals are not handed down from a supernatural God.

Z Quote: *Having killed God, the atheist is left with no reason for being, no morality to espouse, no meaning to life, and no hope beyond the grave. Significantly, the absence of future hope has an amazing capacity to reach into the present and eat away at the structure of life, as termites would a giant wooden foundation.*

Comment: No Atheist has "*killed God*" or any other god. The Christian God is a belief that resides in the minds of Christians. It will live on regardless of what anyone says or does. Atheists seek only to learn about humanity and its relationship to Nature and develop their moral code independent of commands of a supernatural God. Further, Atheists have "*no absence of future hope.*" In fact, it is just the opposite. They believe their studying and research will bring humanity more understanding of the universe and its role in it. These thoughts bring much happiness and hope.

Zacharias misses the fact of the biological evolution of morality—humans have acquired a base morality from the evolutionary process of ancestors. Paul Churchland[19] explains

how moral knowledge, like scientific knowledge, is built from the bottom up over time. Neural networks are formed that can be rewired and tuned to meet new conditions. This allows humans to learn from moral mistakes and correct them. The scientific community successfully used the same approach to build up scientific information a little at a time with continuing corrections.

He further notes that moral knowledge is then *real knowledge precisely because it results from the continual readjustment of our convictions and practices in light of our unfolding experiences of the real world.*

Expanding on this, Patricia Churchland[20] summarizes her understanding of morality:

Morality seems to me to be a natural phenomenon— constrained by the forces of natural selection, rooted in neurobiology, shaped by local ecology, and modified by cultural developments.

She further notes that a naturalistic perspective for the evolution of morals is a great help to

disentangle ourselves from many myths about morality. In disentangling ourselves from the myths, we may become even more keenly aware of our obligation to think a problem through rather than just react blindly or follow a rule.

Education (religious or not) helps to refine one's morality. Christians and believers of other religions contribute to but have no monopoly on morality.

Z Quote: *The atheist believes that one's moral beliefs are a private matter and ought not to impinge upon one's public behavior or surface in one's public pronouncements. Morality is a dirty word in public, and immorality has no damning effect if it is kept private.*

Comment: Atheists have the same concern for private and public morality as Christians. Morality is *not* a dirty word in public, and immorality is to be damned whether private or public. This is true whether an Atheist or Christian perpetrates the impropriety. Further, forcing an either-or decision on imposing God's morals on Atheists and non-Christians runs counter to the Constitution, which presents the workable solution of separating public, secular laws from God's supernaturally imposed laws. All citizens use the common public laws, and Christian citizens are free to also use their God's laws. Thus, morality is *not* a dirty word for Atheists. These are the public laws American citizens imposed on themselves.

Z Quote: *Hitler unintentionally exposed atheism and dragged it where it was reluctantly, but logically, forced into its consequences. The denuding of people, in every sense of the word, that took place in the concentration camps, brought about the logical outworking of the demise of God and the extermination of moral law.*

Comment: Hitler and Stalin were dictators without morals. They were neither atheistic nor religious. In *Mein Kampf*, Hitler declared he was neutral in religious matters[21] but in reality he used any device, including Christianity and Atheism, to control the people and pursue his lust for power. Stalin was the same. Hitler considered all who did not fit his definition of the German Aryan race sinful enemies. Scientifically, he did not know what an Aryan was. He used it as a label to separate people he did not like from those he did.

Hitler did not turn away from Christian recognition. The first organization to recognize him when he came to power was the Catholic Church, which continued its recognition throughout the war. This lack of moral recognition by Christians of an evil organization doing evil acts tarnished the moral leadership of the Vatican. This tacit collaboration between Pope Pius XII and the Nazis has been well documented in books, such as *Papal Sin*[22] and *Hitler's Pope*.[23]

Zacharias presents a number of false assertions about the immorality of Atheists. This includes trying to link Atheists with Hitler and the Nazi concentration camps. Zacharias's failed logic is as follows: Mass murder is evil. Hitler was evil and not a practicing Christian. Hitler, therefore, must be an evil Atheist. Evil dictator? Yes. War mongering psychopath? Yes. Atheist? No. Evil does not reside exclusively in Christians or Atheists.

Cosmology

D'Souza expands his arguments against the evildoers harming Christianity to argue that the secular natural sciences of biology and cosmology actually support the supernatural Christian narrative. God created the universe and fine-tuned it for human life.

> _D'S Quote_: _The latest discoveries of modern science support the Christian claim that there is a divine being that created the universe._

> _D'S Quote_: _Fantastic though it seems, the universe is fine-tuned for human habitation. We live in a kind of Goldilocks universe in which the conditions are "just right" for life to emerge and thrive._

Comment: Again, D'Souza invents a far-out assertion—natural science supports the Christian supernatural claim that there is a divine being that created the universe. Since there is no experimental cosmological data to support this assertion, surely D'Souza knows scientists are not going to support his claims. He nevertheless ventures forth with arguments for God fine-tuning the universe. Most scientists argue that Nature created the universe, and by luck, humans happened to evolve.

Although not all of the details, causes, and mechanics of the universe's creation are known, modern science does have some interesting clues about this creation that are within the bounds of the Standard Model of physics—the laws scientists use to explain Nature without the intervention of a supernatural God.

The Christian claim for God fine-tuning the universe is clearly a supernatural assertion involving a supernatural designer (God). Believers might use this to keep God involved, but such claims do not satisfy the tests natural science requires to establish a credible scientific theory. Natural science simply does not support supernatural divine claims, because there are no data supporting the actions of any supernatural God regarding the creation, design, or fine-tuning of the universe or humans. Scientists reject the fine-tuning argument as another "designed by an Intelligent Designer (God)" argument.

D'Souza fails to remember that the Bible gives a "divine creation of the universe" story with three levels—the Earth at the center, the heavens above, and an underworld below. Five hundred years ago, Copernicus disproved this Christian pseudo-science theory of the Earth as the center of the universe. The theory of a heaven above and an underworld below was similarly disproved. Astronomical telescopes are pretty good these days, and they have yet to find evidence to support the theory that the Earth is at the center of a three-tiered universe.

If D'Souza wants to support the "fine-tuned by a Christian God" theory, he should propose an experiment to prove it. Without data, the Christian divine creation story is only one of many supernatural religious creation stories. Does D'Souza suggest rejecting five hundred years of scientific advances and returning to the belief that the Earth is the center of a universe fine-tuned by divine design?

D'Souza is not alone. In a talk in late 2014, Pope Francis attempted to inject his supernatural God into the secular Big Bang theory.

The Big Bang, which today we hold to be the origin of the world, does not contradict the intervention of the divine creator but, rather, requires it.

Science's understanding of the Big Bang conflicts with the biblical descriptions of creation which start with in the beginning God created the heavens and the Earth. Science says that it was eight billion years after the beginning that the Earth was formed. The pope does not address what God was doing while he waited eight billion years to start forming the Earth.

The Big Bang is a secular theory that does not require a God. Injecting God into this secular theory only illustrates that the Catholic Church is stuck halfway the between biblical creation story and secular theories. This is the same unsatisfactory halfway position the Vatican has on Darwin's Theory. At the general level, it expresses acceptance, but ignores the details that expose the conflicts between the natural world and the supernatural world.

In cosmology, scientists have come a long way in their understanding of the universe. They have strong evidence that the universe was created some 13.7 billion years ago from a Big Bang and not from a Steady State,, the leading theory fifty years ago. Some data have been collected that supports the Big Bang theory. This includes the image of the cosmic microwave background (CMB) radiation emitted about four hundred thousand years after the inflationary phase from the rapidly expanding energy sphere from the bang. Another source of data is recent preliminary measurements of the polarization of the CMB radiation. These data indicate it has been polarized by gravitational waves from the inflationary expansion period fractions of a microsecond after the Big Bang. More data is needed to substantiate these findings, but to date the Standard Model of physics does not seem violated by what has been observed in Nature.

Strong support of the Big Bang comes from calculations of the nucleosynthesis of the elements in universe occurring from the Big Bang using the Standard Model and its agreement with the observational data.

There is still much to learn. As physicists get more data on the Big Bang, there might be a need for new physics theories to explain the mysterious quantum singularity at the beginning of the Big Bang and other unknowns such as dark energy, dark matter, and the state of matter and energy at the center of black holes. It is an exciting time in physics, but so far there is not a job opening for a theologian on the physics team researching the creation of the universe.

Both Zacharias and D'Souza promote a supernatural God as the creator of the universe by "*an intelligent first cause,*" another label for Intelligent Designer.

Z Quote: *The first cause of the creation of the universe is a thorn in the side of the scientists who hold to automatic evolution, rather than an intelligent first cause.*

Comment: Theorizing about the Big Bang's creation of the universe is not a thorn for scientists. It is just a big, deep physics problem for physicists to solve and one in which they are deeply involved. However, it is a thorn in the side of theists. The Big Bang created the space-time of the universe, and as far as scientists can determine, no supernatural God has been detected in the universe so far.

The theological argument of an intelligent first cause is given in the first biblical passage:

In the beginning God created the heavens and the earth.

This is part of the biblical supernatural creation story that scientists reject for many reasons.

Consider the timing. It conflicts with science, for the heavens are some 14.7 billion years old today and with its on-going expansion the heavens are continuing to be formed. The Earth was created 9 billion years after the beginning. The very first sentence of the Bible, therefore, is in conflict with Nature's creation. A supernatural first-cause story of the creation of the universe might be useful in religious narratives and sermons, but natural science theories do not support it.

Z Quote: Polkinghorne notes that scientists have felt particularly uneasy about the balance required by the anthropic principle.

Comment: Some Christians, including priest and scientist John Polkinghorne, believe the explanation of the balance of physical parameters used in describing the universe to be the work of an Intelligent Designer (God), who, according to the Christian theory known as the anthropic principle, set the constants of Nature to support life after God created it. However, most scientists are not uneasy when considering the balance of the physical constants mentioned. If the constants and laws were different, scientists would not have our known universe to worry about. What scientists do have is the observed universe that Nature has given them, and they do that observation with great interest. Although books[24] have been written on the subject expounding the anthropic theory, no experimental data has been produced to add credibility to the subject.

Z Quote: Renowned Cambridge professor Stephen Hawking, for example, is commended for his gift in using the technical data of his expertise to explain the nature of the universe in a popular treatment. However, it does not take long for the reader to realize that the more penetrating the question, the more Hawking's answers elude even the highly trained.

Comment: If one is not a scientist, one should be cautious when criticizing Stephen Hawking's scientific contributions to cosmology. His scientific peers know his work well, and many have contributed to and in some cases critiqued his many scientific papers, books, and lectures.[25] Few scientists would agree with Zacharias's statement that *"Hawking's answers elude even the highly trained."* His fellow physicists and many in the general public understand his contributions to cosmology. It might be that Hawking's answers are simply ones Zacharias does not want to address because Hawking is an Atheist, and his answers do not include God in his scientific theories on the creation or workings of the universe.

Hawking is widely respected in the scientific community as well as the world at large. That respect extends to the general public. One of his books, *A Brief History of Time,* was a bestseller. Not many scientific books do that well.

At Cambridge, Zacharias had the chance to learn about cosmology from many leading professors there. That included the Atheist Stephen Hawking, but obviously, he did not take advantage of that opportunity.

Z Quote: Atheism has never meaningfully defused these questions that force atheistic worldviews into circular arguments. Indeed, addressing the atheist, biologist George Beadle raised the question, "Whence came the hydrogen?" Beadle added, "Is it any less awe-inspiring to conceive of a universe created of hydrogen with the capacity to evolve into man, than it is to accept the

Creation of man as man?" Beadle's point is well-taken. In pushing back the regressive causes, the atheist is not able to escape the inexplicability of an impersonal first cause, to say nothing of the awe-inspiring capacity of the "raw material" from whence it all "evolved." The turning of hydrogen into thinking and purposive beings is scientifically undemonstrated, and philosophically devoid of merit.

<u>Comment</u>: George Beadle, a respected geneticist and Nobel Prize winner, raised the question in 1958 of where the raw material (hydrogen—the primary element in the formation of the universe) came from. In the fifty or so years since that time, an understanding of the Big Bang theory has emerged. This addresses the creation and evolution of hydrogen as well as the elemental abundance of all the other elements in the universe. Calculations using the Standard Model in physics and the measurements made on the distribution of the elements in the universe support this theory.

Today physicists[26] are in general agreement that after the Big Bang, the energy from the explosive expansion began to cool and allowed matter to begin to form. First it was quarks, then protons, and then electrons. These combined with protons to form the simplest atom—hydrogen. Further cooling gave a little of heavier elements lithium and beryllium, but the most prevalent element in the early moments of the universe was hydrogen. All other atoms known today were formed in thermonuclear reactions within stars or in their explosions, which dispersed the elemental material into the universe where stars and planets were subsequently formed.

The planet Earth was formed from the elements in the universe, including hydrogen, oxygen, and carbon. After shuffling about for over a billion years molecules and chemical compounds were formed. From these molecules, the first self-replicating molecule was formed and became the basis of all biological life. Evolution from this first ancestor produced the wide diversity of life we see including humans ("*thinking and purposive beings*") some three billion years later.

Most of these outlined steps, except the spark at the beginning of the Big Bang and the first self-replicating molecule, have been scientifically demonstrated and philosophically accepted by the scientific community. Humans are the thinking and purposive children of the Big Bang—13.7 billion years in the making.

Z Quote: Science just does not have knowledge of the beginnings in the genuine sense of the term. It cannot answer the how, much less the why of there being something rather than nothing.

Z Quote: At this moment it seems as though science will never be able to raise the curtain on the mystery of creation. For the scientist who has lived by his faith in the power of reason, the story ends like a bad dream. He has scaled the mountains of ignorance; he is about to conquer the highest peak; as he pulls himself over the final rock, he is greeted by a band of theologians who have been sitting there.

Comment: Today science does not have complete knowledge about the moment of creation of the universe or all its component pieces, such as dark matter and dark energy. The complete explanation is a work in progress. What it does have is circumstantial evidence from several experiments pointing to the Big Bang as the beginning. Scientists may not have all the answers about the mystery of creation, but they have written a draft of the first chapter based on the observations of Nature that does not include any supernatural gods.

D'Souza and Zacharias are not alone in their denial of science. There is a small set of ministers and a few scientists who continue with the belief that the Christian supernatural God is the creator of the universe. This is despite the vast majority of scientists rejecting a supernatural beginning. The billions of believers of other religions also reject the primacy of the Christian God in the creation of the universe. There are a thousand supernatural religious creation stories and one leading natural science theory from which to choose.

Scientists do not believe they have totally "*scaled the mountains of ignorance.*" After all, they do not know the height of the mountain they are climbing, but they do know they have made progress along the path to knowledge with experimental observations providing a base of understanding the creation. At this point scientists look forward and see a lot of work ahead to get to the next peak in their journeys of understanding Nature. When they look backward, they see many theologians still chained to their two-thousand-year-old ideology that keeps them from making any progress. Some refuse to accept the new and join with the scientific community to look forward and climb the next foothill in the "*mountains of ignorance*" together.

Democracy

D'Souza misrepresents what the Founding Fathers achieved when they established America's secular constitutional government. Until the American experiment with democracy, theocracies throughout the world had coupled religion with government. This combination had produced many countries that engaged in religious wars. The Christian theocracy was the norm for European governments. The Founding Fathers knew the history of the bloody religious wars between Protestant and Catholic theocracies over centuries throughout Europe and sought to avoid them.

The Founding Fathers believed that to have religious freedom, it was necessary to have the American government be separate from religion. No one religion could hold a special place over all other religions. Religious liberty for all people depended on having a secular government. Atheists, Deists, and Unitarians were some of the early leaders in breaking from the British government and its entrenched Anglican religion and establishing a secular American constitution.

Jefferson's letter to Alexander von Humboldt, a Prussian naturalist, stated the case for free civil governance over theocracies:

> *History, I believe, furnishes no example of a priest-ridden people maintaining a free civil government.*

Religious freedom in America was not a gift from the Christian God, as D'Souza and President George Bush have declared. The Christian church cannot be expected to be supportive of secular democratic governments in which all religions and non-religions are treated equally. In fact, the Vatican, with its history of involvement in theocratic governments, had a difficult time accepting the democratic view of religious freedom as late as the mid-1800s. At that time, the Vatican was still arguing that the best form of government was a Catholic theocracy.

The Baptists in England had long been a minority religion and had a long history of arguing for separating religion from the government. As early as 1612, they wrote to the king of England,

> *The magistrate [king] is not by virtue of his office*
> *to meddle with religion, or matters of conscience.*

In 1801 the American Baptists, also a minority religion in America, wrote President Jefferson rejoicing in his election and his support for the separation of church and state affirming that

> *our Sentiments are uniformly on the side of*
> *Religious Liberty.*

President Jefferson answered by summarized the relationship between religion and the American democratic government in his famous letter to the Danbury Baptist Association.

> *Believing with you that religion is a matter which*
> *lies solely between man and his God…I con-*
> *template with sovereign reverence that act of the*
> *whole American people which declared that their*
> *legislature should "make no law respecting an*
> *establishment of religion, or prohibiting the free*
> *practice thereof," thus building a wall of separa-*
> *tion between church and state.*

This metaphor of the wall of separation between church and state is difficult for some Fundamentalists to accept. They have instituted lawsuits to modify or remove the wall, and supporters have brought lawsuits to retain the wall. Pressure on congressmen, senators and even presidents has continued over the years to have Christianity recognized in the federal constitution. Even Abraham Lincoln, one of the most religiously skeptical president since Thomas Jefferson, was approached during the Civil War period to insert a paragraph of the recognition of God into the Constitution, but he dropped the idea late in the war. Although both sides in the Civil War prayed to the same God for victory in the end it was the country without God in its Constitution that won the war.

Several state constitutions do have some form of recognition of God. These have continued to cause problems for maintaining the wall even after the Supreme Court ruled in 1961 against the Maryland's Constitution which said that people who do not believe in God are not eligible to hold public office. Maryland and six other states still have similar articles in their constitutions.

Since approval of the US Constitution Christians have continued their efforts to insert God into the government. Seven example lawsuits on the separation of church and state that the Supreme Court has heard over the last fifty years are listed in appendix E, Defining the Wall of Separation. These Supreme Court suits help to define the wall separating the state from religion regarding certain Christian actions, such as school-endorsed prayer and installations of the Roman cross or Ten Commandments in public schools and on public land. More lawsuits are expected in the continuing struggle over the height and breadth of the constitutional wall separating the church from the state.

Another point of conflict for Christians has been the use of biblical law in America. Secularists argue that the laws the new country adopted were based on English common law— not Christian canon law. As Thomas Jefferson noted,

We may safely affirm that Christianity neither is,
nor ever was, a part of the common law.

His reasoning was straightforward. Early English Common Law could be traced to before the Norman Conquest. Afterward British monarchs added laws to the existing common law. Over time the democratic institutions of British government evolved through a series of power struggles between the king and the people's parliament.

However, England remains a theocracy, with the king being the head of the Church of England, The democratic view that citizens should have the liberty to practice any religion and worship any God (or no God) was a personal freedom that had to wait until the establishment of America's secular constitutional government.

D'S Quote: _The genius of the American founders was to go beyond tolerance to insist that the central government stay completely out of the business of theology. Despite its novelty, this idea was a profoundly Christian one; they were following Christ's rule to keep the domains of Caesar and God separate._

Comment: D'Souza's attempt to argue that the separation of church and state was a Christian idea is fiction. It clearly fails the test of history, as history reveals the opposite. The Christian Church has a two-thousand-year history of being part of theocracies in which they fought for and mostly succeeded in having religion in control of governments. The Papal State today is a theocracy.

It was not beyond tolerance for the Founding Fathers to separate religion from government, because it is not possible to have a democracy guided by a church with a supernatural God in charge. That is what a theocracy does. Jesus might have told his local group of Christians to "render unto Caesar," but after the Roman Emperor Constantine brought Christianity into his government in AD 325, all Christian governments in Europe from then to the democracy experiment in America were Christian theocracies with religious freedom only for Christians—certainly not Jews or Atheists. Citizens in theocracies were told that the law of the land is to "render unto God and Caesar."

The majority of the Founding Fathers were Christian, but several key ones were Atheists, Deists, or Unitarians. This included the first six presidents (Washington, Adams, Jefferson, Madison, Adams, and Monroe) and the first presidential advisor, Franklin, was as well. Clearly, the

authority of the Constitution was its citizens, and it
made no reference to the Christian God or Jesus.
According to Abraham Lincoln, the Constitution
was a document

of the people, by the people and for the people.

Since the Constitution allowed for the equality
of many different religious persuasions, it had to
be a secular constitution to encompass all people
and each of their religions. The First Amendment
established the separation of church and state.

Having theology out of the business of government is a problem for D'Souza. He might
complain, but this separation was Jefferson and
Madison's goal from their early days in the Virginia
state congress. They carried the concept forward
and implemented the separation at the federal
level with the US Constitution.

The Founding Fathers in no way denied the
Christian heritage of most of the citizens. Even
Jefferson, perhaps the least orthodox Christian of
them all, argued that religious faith was a right of
each citizen and was generally helpful for the citizens personally. However, the Founding Fathers
steadfastly voted to keep religion separate from
the government.

*D'S Quote: After the Revolutionary War, the founders
continued to hold public days of prayer, to appoint chaplains for Congress and the armed forces, and to promote
religious values through the schools in the Northwest
Territory.*

Comment: This is generally true. It took some
time to determine where religious customs and
the establishment of the separation of church met.
Many of these early governmental actions were
largely ceremonial, and although some continue

today, most have changed or dropped. Although Washington and Adams had a national day of prayer, Jefferson decided not to have one while he was president. Madison allowed it again but said in reflection it was a mistake. Subsequently presidents define national days.

Education under the Northwest Ordinance[27] was a temporary act that was replaced by secular public schools when public education became a national mandate. All schools thereafter operated under the constitutional ruling that public schools were to be secular, and government-funded education could not promote one religion's values over all others.

In our democracy laws continue to change with shifting social mores and political environment. There are now Muslim and Atheist representatives in Congress, and no longer are the chaplains in Congress and the military only Protestant Christians but some are from other religions and belief systems. The national cemetery at Arlington, Virginia, originally had only Christian tombstones with Christian crosses for all soldiers that died. It now recognizes fifty-six different religious headstones, so soldiers no longer suffer religious discrimination at the hands of the government upon burial.

Because of the strong feelings on both sides on the wall separating church and state, that wall is continually tested. Exactly where the wall is located and how what its hight is are continuing legal arguments that have resulted in many lawsuits concerning specific attempts to inject religion into the public area. Legal arguments on the constitutional wall will likely continue into the future as each new generation seeks to interpret the Constitution within the context of their religion.

D'S Quote: Today courts wrongly interpret separation of church and state to mean that religion has no place in the public arena, or that morality derived from religion should not be permitted to shape our laws. Somehow freedom for religious expression has become freedom from religious expression. Secularists want to empty the public square of religion and religious-based morality so they can monopolize the shared space of society with their own views. In the process they have made religious believers into second-class citizens. This is a profound distortion of a noble idea that is also a Christian idea. The separation of the realms should not be a weapon against Christianity; rather, it is a device supplied by Christianity to promote social peace, religious freedom, and a moral community. If we recovered the concept in its true sense, our society would be much better off.

Comment: Every assertion in this paragraph of twisted logic is incorrect. The most far-out invented assertion is that "*the separation of the realms…is a device supplied by Christianity to promote social peace, religious freedom, and a moral community.*"

For 1,500 years the Christian Church was the dominant member of theocracies that allowed no separation of the church and state. Social peace occurred only when Jews and Atheists were periodically tolerated, but the norm was that Jews and Atheists were the subjects of attacks. The Jewish community was at a disadvantage in that it was more visible. The Jewish members openly professed their faith and built synagogues for services. The Atheist could just be silent and escape prosecution, but being silent is often difficult and does not always work.

Theocracies determined the morals of the community through laws that favored one religion, and one religion's control never brought social peace or community morals to any country. In fact, Christian theocracies, both Catholic and Protestant, were involved in many religious wars with little social peace achieved. The separation of church and state is not a *"weapon against Christianity."* It is a constitutional precept necessary for the secular democracy our Founding Fathers promoted. The Constitution protects all religions from governmental interference and separates the government from religious intrusion.

Religious-based morality can be suggested by believers of any religion, but to be part of a law, a majority of the citizens (who can be expected to be of many different religions) must approve it. It is the will of the people and not the will of a religion that determines the laws of a democracy and defines the moral community.

Today at the federal level all religions have a place in the public arena, and Christians are not second-class citizens any more than any other citizen. However, the states have their own constitutions which define Atheists as second-class citizens. As noted before the State of Maryland and six other states still have articles in their constitutions[28] saying people who do not believe in God are not eligible to hold public office. D'Souza has it backward, it is the Atheists not the Christians who are being treated as second-class citizens.

The history of Christianity's intrusion into America's secular government is a tangled mess, and the extent of the mess has varied over time as political forces and government officials with different religious intensities have changed. This can be seen by the depth of the belief of each president. For example, there was minimal intrusion of religion into government with the first five presidents—Washington, Adams, Jefferson, Madison, and Monroe. They were Atheists, Deists, or Unitarians. Since then, all presidents have been Protestants, except for John Kennedy, who was Catholic. Being the first non-Protestant president, he took great care to honor the separation of church and state. However, in the last fifty years, there have been Christian intrusions, and the most intrusions by far were under the presidency of born-again Christian George Bush. Bush never accepted the separation of church and state or the secular base of America's democracy. He famously said,

therefore democracy—being not just America's gift to the world but [the Christian] God's gift to mankind.

Bush further declared people had inalienable rights,

because they bear the image of the [Christian] Maker of heaven and earth.

Bush's inalienable rights differed in word and spirit from those of Jefferson in the Declaration of Independence. Jefferson wrote,

Men are endowed by their Creator with certain unalienable rights…that to secure these Rights, governments are instituted among men, deriving their just powers from the Consent of the Governed.

The Founding Fathers did not think democracy was a gift given by a supernatural God. It was the result of the blood, sweat, and tears of its citizens. As Jefferson noted, the governed were Atheists, Deists, Unitarians, Christians, and believers of other religions. These non-Christians would not agree that their images were given to them by the Christian God or that their rights came from having Christian images.

Knowing there has been a decline of Christian primacy in laws and science over the years, Christians would do well to remember the real reasons for the decline. Government and science have become independent of religion in America. Christians must acknowledge that American democratic laws have evolved from kingly English common law of the past. The many steps in the evolution of our democracy include the Magna Carta, a rebellion by English nobles, and the rise of parliamentary power to limit the powers of the king to impose laws. They also include the American Revolution, which established a constitution instituted by the people and for the people to make the laws. One of those laws separated religions from the government.

Over the 230 years of American democracy, the source of morality has been the citizens. They enact democratic laws that define the country's collective social morality. Christians might receive gifts from their God, but it is hardly possible that the Christian God gave gifts to Atheists and other non-Christians who also helped bring democracy to American shores.

Secular Education

D'Souza has a rather negative view of secular public education, but he offers no specific alternative. Does he really want a Christian-centered religious education in public schools?

D'S Quote: It seems that atheists are not content with committing cultural suicide—they want to take your children with them. The atheist strategy can be described in this way: let the religious people breed them, and we will educate them to despise their parents' beliefs. So the secularization of the minds of our young people is not, as many think, the inevitable consequence of learning and maturing. Rather, it is to a large degree orchestrated by teachers and professors to promote anti-religious agendas.

Comment: This is indeed a remarkably anti-democratic, anti-intellectual view of public education. Americans have long been proud of the early introduction and support of secular public education at the state and national level. One might ask how one can otherwise educate the citizens of many different religious persuasions in a democracy if not by secular public schools. Therefore, it is not only Atheists who support secular education but citizens of all religions who know if public education is to be for all it must be free, secular, and treat everyone the same in their education.

Only the extreme Fundamentalists object to secular public education. They want their children to have only their religion's instructions. Families have the freedom to provide the religious segment of children's education through church-supported schools.

Surely D'Souza is aware of the difficulties trying to teach non-secular subjects in public school. Take natural science as an example. Within Christianity and other religions, there is a spectrum of acceptance of science. There are Fundamentalist Christians who would argue that schools should teach biblical literalism that the Earth is seven thousand years old. Scientists, Atheists, and most Christians would disagree and argue to have the scientific age of 4.5 billion years taught. Fundamentalist Christians are free to believe and teach whatever age of the Earth they want in their church schools but not in public schools, where natural science is the standard.

Atheists and scientists have no reason to have anti-Christian views, because science is apolitical. If teaching secular science bothers Christians, the Christian biblical viewpoint based on supernatural pseudo-science is the problem. Teaching that the Earth is billions of years old is not anti-Christian. It is a natural science fact based on radioactive dating measurements.

The majority of citizens, including a Christian majority, do not want biblical pseudo-science taught in science classes. They want natural science taught because they want their children to be educated so they can compete in the secular world. The supernatural religious view can be taught in church schools if Christians choose.

History

D'Souza asserts that a major theme of the Atheist discourse is their focus on recounting the historical crimes of Christianity. Past crimes by Christian leaders and institutions are part of history, and killing people in the name of God is not limited to Christians. Many other religions have done so and are doing so today. Christians, though, do share in killings over history. The Vatican's Inquisition, the Christian Crusades, the Christian religious wars, and the Christian witch trials are events where Christians were the leaders, and many deaths resulted. They are as much a part of history as the mass killings by non-Christians. All such killings are morally wrong whether performed by Christians or non-Christians, but people can learn only if they are remembered and taught in schools. The general moral indictment from history is that when people and institutions (Christian or non-Christian) seek power and are unchecked, that power is often used to kill opponents. The greater the power, the greater the killings, and the Christian Church has certainly had great power over a large number of people over many years.

History's moral indictment of Christians along with non-Christians for religious killings is a fact D'Souza does not want to hear. It would force him to acknowledge that the morality of Christian organizations and their theocracies have over history has been generally the same as that of non-Christians.

Galileo Revisited

To provide an example of his second theme, D'Souza revisits the 1633 trial of Galileo by the Vatican's Inquisition as an illustration of how Atheist writers have attempted to show the evils of the Church. Christian and secular historians have amply documented Galileo's trial in 1633 and that period of time in which Church theocracies had the power to accuse, jail, and kill people for the crime of heresy—a charge they could define as anything that conflicted with the Church's dogma. When the Vatican believed Galileo's writings conflicted with the Vatican's pseudo-science dogma (that the Earth was at the center of the universe), it defended its dogma by placing Galileo on trial.

The Vatican decided that Galileo had violated its dogma through the geocentric theory of the universe and by conducting experiments and writing about a secular theory—Copernicus's heliocentric theory—as a replacement for its dogma in his 1632 book,[29] *Dialogue Concerning the Two Chief World Systems.* The pope at the time, Urban VIII, was once friendly with Galileo but never forgave him for including in his book discussions of God's power from the character Simplicio—a character whose arguments in the book were poorly made.

The Vatican's Inquisition brought Galileo to trial for heresy in 1633. The Church served as the judge, prosecutor, and jury and proceeded to find him guilty not of bad science but of religious heresy. The Church could have taken many actions against the elderly Galileo, but it pressed ahead with his trial, found him guilty of being a "suspect of heresy," and put him under house arrest for the rest of his life.

Galileo's book discussing the Church's dogma and Copernicus's book were put on the Vatican's index of prohibited books. It remained there for 125 years. However, Galileo's work and his book had already been disseminated into the scientific community, which eagerly studied his work as it had with Copernicus's earlier theory. In 1992 the Vatican admitted it had made a mistake and had come to the wrong verdict in the Galileo trial. Surely, taking 359 years to reverse a trial's verdict is a record for any bureaucracy.

D'Souza takes Galileo's trial and rewrites it with false assertions that paint Galileo as a pushy old scientist who had little common sense. It recasts the involved members of the Vatican's Inquisition as reasonable and considerate clergy. With these new characters, D'Souza rewrites history and arrives at new and false implications of the trial.

D'S Quote: Galileo was a great scientist who had very little sense. He was right about heliocentrism, but several of his arguments and proofs were wrong. The dispute his ideas brought about was not exclusively between religion and science, but also between the new science and the science of the previous generation. The leading figures of the church were more circumspect about approaching the scientific issues, which were truly unsettled at the time, than the impetuous Galileo. The church should not have tried him, but his trials were conducted with considerable restraint and exemplary treatment. The leading figures of the church were more circumspect about approaching the scientific issues, which were truly unsettled at the time, than the impetuous Galileo.

Comment: D'Souza's version of history has Galileo, in his view, deservedly being punished and the Church's pseudo-science and moral reasoning elevating the Church to be the "good guys," doing only what they had to do under the circumstances. D'Souza casts the leading figures of the Church to be "*more circumspect about approaching the scientific issues than Galileo*" and indicates that being circumspect is more important than getting the science right. This is not an argument accepted by scientists but a blatant attempt to rewrite history and whitewash the Church's actions against science and the scientist.

D'Souza is not the first apologist to argue that the Church acted properly, punishing Galileo with the information available at the time. Cardinal Ratzinger (later Pope Benedict XVI) argued the same in 1990 when he said, "*[The Vatican's] verdict against Galileo was rational and just.*" In 2008 the same pope had to cancel a trip to La Sapienza University in Rome after this comment on Galileo surfaced and created much protest from the scientists at the university. The university's physics department (all ninety-five members) threatened to boycott the event, and the pope canceled the trip. D'Souza's attempt to rewrite the history of the Galileo trial is an example of his disdain for history and should be challenged.

The Galileo trial was not an isolated affair for the Vatican to defend its dogma. The Vatican had already condemned the infinite universe theory of Epicurus before the Galileo case. The priest Giordano Bruno presented this idea even though it conflicted with the Vatican's pseudo-science theory of a finite three-region Earth-centered universe. Supporting Epicurus' theory was enough for Bruno to be accused of heresy.

Just as Galileo's science has been proven right, so has Bruno's. The Church could have understood that science was advancing and new theories were worth considering. Instead it chose to defend the old official dogma and attack the scientist and philosopher bringing the new science. For Bruno, it was death by burning at the stake. For Galileo, it was house arrest for the remainder of his life.

Proselytizing and Politics

In addition to attacking Atheist evildoers, D'Souza turns to Christian proselytizing to conclude his book. That is fine, but when the arguments revert to pushing fear (you are going to hell if you do not agree with me), he has lost the high ground of reason.

D'S Quote: *You must choose God or reject Him, because when you die all abstentions are counted as "no" votes. So if you are wondering if this book is an invitation to convert, it is. I hope you will read it as if your life depended on it, because, in a way, it might.*

Comment: It is not expected this argument will win over many of the Atheists he has attacked as evildoers and who are already heading to hell. Other non-Christians might recognize the attacks made on Atheists and think they might be next in line.

During the Obama presidential campaign, D'Souza used the same techniques in another book—false assumptions to develop political attacks on the opposing party's candidate, Obama. D'Souza expanded a brief interview[30] with Obama's father into an invented argument that was included in a book about Obama's thoughts. D'Souza, however, had never actually talked to Obama.

D'S Quote: Barack Obama's attitude toward America derives from his father's anti-colonialism and from a psychological desire to fulfill his father's dream of diminishing the power of Western imperial states.

Comment: Critics contend that D'Souza's arguments (based on his short interview with Obama's father) contain conspiracy, speculation, and projection. This is the same approach used for disparaging Atheists. Any verification of D'Souza's assertions of Obama's attitude would have to come from the president, and that has not been done. By default, therefore, D'Souza's unsupported inventions are left dangling and unresolved in the public mind. The same is true for the Atheists, who have been attacked by negative assertions left unsubstantiated.

Closing

Zacharias ends with a few comments that show his discomfort with God missing from the discourse on science engaged in by Atheists and scientists.

Z Quote: To be an intellectual is a great privilege, but to be an intellectual without God is dangerous.

Comment: This viewpoint is unsubstantiated. There have been and are now many godless intellectuals, scientists, and Atheists who are not dangerous and have made substantial contributions to humankind. These intellectuals extend over time and range from Epicurus to Thomas Jefferson to Steven Hawking. Zacharias would have a hard time convincing anyone these people have been dangerous.

Zacharias's comment is similar to another blanket statement that has been around for a while—there are no Atheists in foxholes. This also has no basis in reality, but it makes for a snappy comment.

Z Quote (from G. K. Chesterton): *Truth, of course, must be stranger than fiction, for we have made fiction to suit ourselves.*

Comment: In the godless science of quantum mechanics,[31] scientists would agree the science theories are far stranger than any fiction humans or any God could have invented. The theories are so strange no self-respecting God would want to claim them. For many the Big Bang theory of creation of the universe from nothing falls into that category.

5

FINAL NOTES

BEFORE ANSWERING THE question posed in the title of this book, *Atheist, Friend or Foe?*, the world view of Atheists is summarized. It is far different from the one assumed by D'Souza and Zacharias on which they based their attacks.

Atheist World View

The following ideas summarize the Atheist world view as seen by a scientist:

1. Natural science is a product of the observation of Nature. It is incompatible with supernatural gods and religions.
2. The universe is a product of Nature which we view through scientific explorations. The Big Bang and subsequent natural science theories describe what we have learned about the physical evolution its matter and forces. u.
3. *Homo sapiens* or man is a product of biological evolution, described by Darwin's Theory of natural selection from a common ancestor. The diversity and complexity of life is explainable by natural processes.

4. Supernatural religions and gods are inventions of humans and do not require experimental verification. They provide spiritual guidance to believers and humanitarian services to many. Religions are incompatible with natural science and secular governance and should be practiced separately.

5. The partnership of religions, natural science, and our secular constitutional democracy provides freedom for its citizens when there is a separation of the authorities of each of the three independent disciplines.

The difference between what D'Souza and Zacharias write about and what Atheists believe is an over reliance on Christian ideology coupled with an under reliance on research of what Atheists think.

Friend or Foe?

The books by the Christian apologists, D'Souza and Zacharias, are basically sermons attacking the evildoing foes of Christianity—the Atheists. This is not new for Atheists have long been labeled evildoers from the very early days of Christianity. Their books update the old militant Christian attacks.

Atheists understand they are not alone on the receiving end of such attacks. Historically, outsiders of all types have also been declared foes by Christians. Consider the Pagans and the Jews, who suffered not only from their first pogrom by Christians in AD 38 in Alexandria but many times afterward. In Europe, Christian-led pogroms killed Jews in large numbers in Trier during the First Crusade in 1096. The Nazis led the last in that city in 1944 during the Holocaust.

D'Souza and Zacharias do not see Atheists as individuals with differing thoughts for they are portrayed with a single identity, one that threatens Christendom. Are these writers so insecure that they believe Christianity cannot face critical thinking by a minority with a different religious opinion from theirs? Why is having no God scarier than believers with competing gods?

The attacks on Atheists are primarily by Fundamentalists and are centered on categories of people (scientists, educators, philosophers and writers) who are declared as evildoers associated with the advance of modernity that conflict with passages in the Christian God's supernatural Bible. Fundamentalists seek to have God's "truths" prevail over Nature's "truths" as well as the "truths" of other religions. If their Bible says the first humans (Adam and Eve) were created fully formed seven thousand years ago, that is all Fundamentalist need to know on that subject. Other views are to be attacked as heresies. Once the biblical God's "truths" are allowed to supersede Nature's "truths" the door is opened for a broad range of conflicting natural science theories to be opposed: in geology (the Earth is 4.5 billion years old), in physics (radioactive dating measures back billions of years), and in human evolution (*Homo sapiens* appeared about two hundred thousand years ago).

Atheists also note that if biblical supernatural stories, such as the Adam and Eve creation story, even though they are inventions of man are kept in the supernatural world of religion there is no conflict for scientists simply do not address supernatural stories. Such stories have long been used in sermons over thousands of years in almost every culture. The Christian biblical tales of Adam and Eve, Noah's worldwide flood, and other tales have a place in biblical sermons where the supernatural is an integral part of the narrative.

D'Souza's and Zacharias's books do not seek workable solutions to the conflicts by separating the invented supernatural from the observed natural theories, but instead attempt to solve the conflicts by imposing biblical "truths" on natural science "truths". The tragedy for Fundamentalist

Christians is that their theocratic authority over natural science and governance has long been lost. The successful scientific revolution over the last five hundred years cannot be turned back. In the West natural science that underpins the modern, secular worldview hasbecome established and has become far too robust and useful to too many that even clever Christian apologists cannot dislodge the scientific "truths".

Attempting to hold to old religious pseudo-science dogma by attacking Atheists and scientists and their theories only exposes the Christian writers to either their lack of understanding of natural science in today's world or their deliberate use of false theories. This is particularity apparent (and appalling) with the multiple attacks by both writers on Darwin's Theory. Surely Zacharias knows Darwin's Theory is embraced as a fact by the biology department at Cambridge University where he went to school.

Despite Fundamentalists' beliefs and wishes our understanding of Nature marches onward as we learn more about how: cells multiply following their DNA instructions, natural selection acts on individual life-forms, and new species continue to be created and struggle for survival. The Darwinian process has been working on Earth for 3.5 billion years. Life forms have ranged from the first self-replicating molecules, to the first cell, to the Cambrian explosion of life-forms 5 hundred million years ago, to the age of the dinosaurs 200 hundred million years ago on to the arrival of modern man 200 thousand years ago. Evolution is a universal natural science theory that continues today.

Glimpses of the vast extent and diversity of biological life on this Earth can be seen in museums around the world. However, it appears D'Souza and Zacharias cannot see or hear what the universities teach, what the museums display, or what observatories record from the light gathered by the giant telescopes peering at the billions of stars and galaxies billions of light-years away in the cosmos display for they are blinded by a first-century, supernatural ideology that although useful in religious communities cannot be used to explain the natural world.

Both D'Souza and Zacharias live in America with a multiplicity of religions all of which live under: civil laws by the authority of a constitutional government, natural science theories by the authority of the scientific community, and religious ideologies by the authority of the many churches. Christians are free to have their own church-based religious ideology separate from the governmental laws and natural science theories. They are free to use their supernatural ideology within their faith community as they wish, but they cannot impose it on the public or public institutions.

There are examples of the scientific, religious, and governmental agencies working in small religious communities such as the Amish, who have adjusted to the reality of the separation of the three. By belief the Amish reject some items of modernity, such as photos, cameras, telephones, and automobiles, but they do not impose their view on others outside of their communities. Their neighbors are not foes—only friends with different beliefs. The Amish are good neighbors to their Christian neighbors, and most Christians are good neighbors to them. However, D'Souza and Zacharias write as if they are developing a manual about how to be bad neighbors by attacking those who are different from them.

Their attacks on natural science also do a disservice to young Christian students who are misled into believing that supernatural biblical pseudo-science used in their religious narratives is acceptable in public school science classrooms. They don't consider how poorly a young Christian student trained in such pseudo-science will fare when put into a public university class where the natural sciences are taught. He or she is placed at a great disadvantage by not being able to understand natural science and compete in the wide secular world that embraces it. Fundamentalist Christians appear not to seek the best education at the best universities for their children.

Through its successes, the scientific community has established science's authority as an independent discipline. Religions are recognized as independent authorities separated from the government by the Constitution, but both are contributors to the marketplace of social, spiritual, and moral philosophies. Both are major providers for the country's humanitarian needs.

Christians, members of the largest of the many religions in the country, must expect to live with the rough-and-tumble contest of ideas in America's dynamic democracy. Some denominations, such as the Progressive Christians, are leading the way for Christians to reconcile their beliefs in Jesus' message with natural science and progressive social issues, such as gay marriage, homosexual equality, and women's rights. Who would have thought gay marriage (social unions many Christian churches have long forbidden) would become legal in many states by popular vote—even in states where Christians are a majority?

Hopefully, Progressive Christians will continue to join with Atheists and lead the effort to reduce the conflicts with other Christians. The breadth and depth of scientific advances are far too extensive and helpful to humanity to turn back the clock and be rejected. Christian apologists would be more helpful to Christianity if they accepted natural science's theories and democracy's separation of church and state and focus their energies on championing Christian contributions to America's humanitarian needs. Their fellow Christians, the Progressives, are leading the way.

Many of D'Souza's and Zacharias's arguments appear as if athey were the last gasp of the flat-Earthers before they have to admit the world is really spherical. Nature's mysteries are not to be feared but brought to light by investigation. This has already illuminated new science explaining how the universe started with a quantum spark that expanded into stars, life was made from the dust of those stars on a small planet circling one star, and a common ancestor many different life-forms evolved by Darwinian natural selection. One created species were the humans who possessed inventive minds that created supernatural God stories. One of those stories embellished the life of Jesus who advocated loving your neighbors—even Atheists–and blossomed into Christianity. The question the title poses can now be answered. Atheists are neighbors like other neighbors with many religions: they are citizens abiding by our country's laws who happen to respect natural science and religious freedoms. Atheists welcome D'Souza and Zacharias as neighbors in the twenty-first century. The breadth of knowledge humans possess will amaze them when they remove their first-century religious blinders and see the world as their fellow Progressive Christians do.

Challenge for Christians

A disturbing observation came from reading D'Souza's and Zacharias's books. The two Christian authors chose not to follow a central message of their religion—love your neighbor. In fact, they chose the opposite, to treat one group, the Atheists, as evildoing outsiders. Ten examples of their attacks on Atheists are listed in appendix D, Quiz on Atheists. One quiz question, number six, reads,

Atheists are spiritually dislodged, estranged from reason, and led into a delirium of vanity?

These three attacking assertions are made without any examples or proofs. The assertions are assumed to apply to all Atheists. There are many examples refuting these assertions. One Atheist previously mentioned, the cosmologist Stephen Hawking, is one Atheist who has never been accused of being "*spiritually dislodged, estranged from reason, and led into a delirium of vanity.*" In fact, his actions have demonstrated just the opposite. Hawking is just one of many who would not fit the accusations.

These false assertions and many others by D'Souza and Zacharias are totally unacceptable in a country where religious freedom is a principle and available to all, believers and non-believers. Some Christians need to find their good angels and extend the message of Jesus to all people of all religions.

These two Christian books attacking Atheists are far different from a book by a Founding Father considered as Atheist talking about Christians. Although Jefferson had some problems with institutional Christianity, the divinity of Jesus, and supernatural miracles in the Bible, he respected Jesus as a person and his moral philosophy, even though he approached Jesus's philosophy differently:

Jesus was a spiritualist and I am a materialist.

Even with this difference, he thought Jesus's morals were gems to be saved and wished to add them to his cache of moral philosophies. He proceeded to save them by editing the Bible and extracting those passages he thought important— primarily the parables and precepts from the Gospels of the New Testament. He pasted these into a blank book and titled it *The Life and Morals of Jesus of Nazareth Extracted Textually from the Gospels in Greek, Latin, French and English.* (appendix, C, Notes on *The Jefferson Bible*)

Later, Jefferson wrote to John Adams that his selections of Jesus's philosophy were easy to recover because they were

as distinguishable as diamonds in a dunghill. [It was]
the most sublime and benevolent code of morals which
has ever been offered to man.

Not extracted were Jesus's miracles, anything supernatural, or Jesus's divinity. He left those to Christians to believe.

What would a book look like if D'Souza and Zacharias did the same as Jefferson but to Atheists books? What would they select for the best of Atheism, natural science, and secular democratic government? Surely some Christian could do this and assemble a comparable book with the "best" of Atheism. A suggested title for such a work would be *The Experiments and Theories of Natural Science and Governance Extracted from Scientific and Government Publications in German, French, Russian, and English*. However, I would be happy with extraction only from English journals For my German, French, and Russian language skills are not too great.

Such a book would allow Christians to appreciate the best in Atheistic thought about Nature's contributions to knowledge in a manner comparable to Jefferson's appreciation of the best of Jesus's moral message. Christians would then have Nature's "truths" to place alongside God's "truths" and, hence have a much broader moral philosophy. The Atheist Jefferson did it. Are there not Christian authors who could do the same?

Toward a Partnership

A partnership of Christians with Atheists, Deists, Unitarians, and believers of all other religions within a rather loose confederation of states brought about the successful American Revolution in the face of a common oppressor. This de facto partnership forged America's independence and established a new democracy by following the leadership and service of Americans without regard to their religious affiliation.

Some of the Atheists, Deists, and Unitarians who answered the call for independence were active heroes— Thomas Young a leader of the original Tea Party in Boston Harbor; Ethan Allen an early war hero for the capture of Fort Ticonderoga; Thomas Paine an early hero for publishing rallying calls for the Revolution; Thomas Jefferson, author of the Declaration of Independence; James Madison steward to the assembly of the Constitution; and Benjamin Franklin the elder sage of the Revolution. In partnership with these leaders, the Christian majority contributed at every step and together they came through many struggles and established the Constitution as the governing document.

Writing books with reckless accusations against a small non-religious segment of citizens (the Atheists, Deists, and Unitarians) damages citizen partnerships with Christians and other Americans who enjoy democracy. The laws of America's secular democracy and the theories of natural science are robust enough that religious attacks accomplish little. Natural science describes the reality of the physical world, democratic government provides personal and religious freedoms for all, and religions provide faith services for the believers.

In matters of natural science, the scientific community has earned its de facto authority as a secular and independent discipline. Religions are free and independent disciplines and may employ supernatural narratives for guidance within their religious communities.

The partnership of Atheists, Deists, Unitarians, and Christians at that singular moment in Revolutionary history gave America an opportunity to establish itself as a secular democracy. Today the Constitution remains a guide for citizens, but it takes the will of Christians, Atheists, and believers of all religions to form a partnership to make the country work. Are there citizens up to the task of continuing the partnership?

Conclusion

Public schools should address the independence[32] of natural science, supernatural religions, and our secular government with its precept to keep religion separate from the government in order that there are personal freedoms for all. The relationship of religion with science also requires separation, for there are no winners in mixing the two: Faith "truths" cannot be imposed on science, or science "truths" on faith. The two are based on separate world views—one supernatural and the other natural. These two views have been around for a long time and are going to be around for a long time in the future. Continuing the partnership among those with many differing religious beliefs in our democracy will allow us to be friends working toward the common goal of freedom and not foes.

Postscript

It is a sad note that Billy Graham, a famous Christian evangelical minister, attached his endorsement to Zacharias's book for the book is a collection of unsupported attacks on a religious minority—the Atheists. Graham's endorsement broadens support of Atheist attacks to many others in the Christian community. Zacharias summarizes his views:

"Atheism—its true nature is despair."

This declaration is pure fiction as the critique of his book has shown. The true nature of most Atheists is hope, not despire.

And for Graham to elevate this falsehood as an answer for anything is troubling. Graham is quoted as saying,

> *If you are looking for an answer to the greatest question of our time, here is a book that faces it head on.*

As a spiritual advisor to several presidents of the United States, it is indeed sad that Graham would have advised presidents that the answer to the greatest question of the present time is to face head on the evils of a religious minority, the Atheists. Is not religious freedom still one of America's founding principles? Are there not greater questions facing the country—such as how to feed and care for the poor, needy, and helpless and how to defend our country today?

Appendix A

**Cambridge University Course—Evolution and Behaviour
A Level Biology[33]**

THIS OPTION COVERS the full range of biology disciplines and lays the foundation for the study of Cell and Developmental Biology, Ecology, Genetics, Plant Sciences, Psychology and Zoology. You're introduced to the major principles of evolutionary theory and explore the origins, evolution and diversity of life on Earth; and major transitions such as the origin of eukaryotes and multi-cellularity using new and fast-evolving methods and techniques.

The second half of the option explores animal behaviour in an evolutionary context, including the evolution of sociality, culture and intelligence; comparative studies of learning and memory; the evolution and behaviour of primates and humans; and evolutionary psychology. You develop practical biological skills through practical classes and a field course.

By the end of the year, we hope that you'll agree with Theodosius Dobzhansky (1900–75) that "nothing in biology makes sense except in the light of evolution."

Appendix B

**Notes on the Biological Evolution of the Human
Eye and Vertebrate Blood Clotting**

BOTH D'SOUZA AND Zacharias refuse to accept Darwin's Theory of natural selection, and in its place, they put forward the long-discredited theory of Intelligent Design as a replacement. This has been championed by Michael Behe and others to explain the evolution of complex human biological systems, such as the human eye and the human blood-clotting system. Fundamentalist Christians claim that both are irreducibly complex and can be explained only by the introduction of God as the supernatural Intelligent Designer—that is, make God the designer of these biological systems, not Nature.

The assertion that a supernatural God is needed as the designer of complex systems has been proven wrong through research by evolutionary biologists. This brief note will address Zacharias's comments on Intelligent Design and the evolution of the human eye and then present an overview of evolutionary biology of one of man's most complex systems, that of blood clotting. This discussion is based on the work described in Russell Doolittle's book *The Evolution of Vertebrate Blood Clotting.*

Human Eye

Zacharias says that Darwin did not address the origin of the human eye. He then turns to Michael Behe's arguments that propose the Intelligent Design theory as a replacement of Darwin's Theory on the origins of the human eye. The facts give a far-different story; Darwin did address the evolution of the human eye in his theory and subsequent research has supported Darwin's Theory. To quote Darwin:[34]

> *If numerous gradations from a simple and imperfect eye to one complex and perfect can be shown to exist, each grade being useful to its possessor, as is certainly the case; if further, the eye ever varies and the variations be inherited, as is likewise certainly the case and if such variations should be useful to any animal under changing conditions of life, then the difficulty of believing that a perfect and complex eye could be formed by natural selection, though insuperable by our imagination, should not be considered as subversive of the theory.*

Since Darwin's publication in 1859, biological research has been able to uncover scientific facts at the genomic and DNA level that describe the evolution of the human eye[35] in detail. Many books and even videos are available with detailed scientific explanations. The Public Broadcasting Service has featured a TV program, *Darwin's Dangerous Idea*, based on a book by Daniel Dennett that presented a summary of the evolution of the human eye:

> *Through natural selection, different types of eyes have emerged in evolutionary history and the human eye isn't even the best one, from some standpoints. Because blood vessels run across the surface of the retina instead of beneath it, it's easy for the vessels to proliferate or leak and impair vision. So, the evolution theorists say, the anti-evolution*

argument that life was created by an "intelligent designer" doesn't hold water: If God or some other omnipotent force was responsible for the human eye, it was something of a botched design.

The Intelligent Design argument goes back many years to a proposal by Reverend Paley in 1805. Darwin's encounter with Paley's theory while at Cambridge is recounted by George Johnson, who summarizes[36] Darwin's initial reaction and his subsequent discarding of it in his lifetime. Darwin, as a student at Cambridge, was required to read Paley's Intelligent Design theory and initially expressed his admiration for the man's clear thinking. Later, Darwin changed his mind and wrote in his autobiography:

> *Again in my last year I worked with some earnestness for my final degree of B.A., and brushed up my classics together with a little algebra and Euclid, which latter gave me much pleasure, as it did whilst at school. In order to pass the B.A. examination, it was, also, necessary to get up Paley's "Evidences of Christianity," and his "Moral Philosophy."… The logic of this book and as I may add of his "Natural Theology" gave me as much delight as did Euclid.…I did not at that time trouble myself about Paley's premises; and taking these on trust I was charmed and convinced by the long line of argumentation.*

Darwin later found a more pleasing explanation for the tension between diversity and order that generates life with his own theory:

> *The old argument of design in nature, as given by Paley, which formerly seemed to me so conclusive, fails, now that the law of natural selection has been discovered. We can no longer argue that, for instance, the beautiful hinge of*

a bivalve shell must have been made by an intel-
ligent being, like the hinge of a door by man.
There seems to be no more design in the vari-
ability of organic beings and in the action of
natural selection, than in the course which the
wind blows. Everything in nature is the result of
fixed laws.

Since Darwin's publication of his theory in 1859, considerable research has placed Darwin's Theory into the category of scientific fact. As stated by the Cambridge Biology Department, one should know as a result of completing its biology courses,

that "nothing in biology makes sense except in the
light of evolution."

The Intelligent Design theory has been relegated to the dustbin of history, which unfortunately gets opened from time to time by those attempting to use it as an alternate to Darwin's Theory.

Blood-Clotting System

Once biological life appeared, there was a continuing demand on each system of the living organism to adapt to the increasing performance demands from evolution to produce new, more active, and more competitive life-forms. One such biological system, blood clotting, evolved to staunch the loss of blood in case of leaks in bodies, which are bound to happen when circulating fluid systems are incorporated into living organisms. The blood-clotting system has evolved to meet the demands of each new species over the last five hundred million years of evolution. For humans, Doolittle notes:

Blood coagulation in humans is a delicately bal-
anced process involving more than two dozen
extracellular proteins, many of which need to be
converted from precursor forms during the process.

Figure B-1 Human Tree of Life illustrates the evolutionary tree of life for over five hundred million years; from early life-forms, such as amphioxus, a fishlike marine chordate appearing in the Cambrian period, to fish, to frogs, and on to humans today.

During the evolution of vertebrates, there was an increasing demand on the clotting system of each new species as the pressure and flow rate of the blood increased. There was a need not only to stop a leak but to localize it at the site of injury, do it quickly, and construct a seal that would keep out harmful microbes. New blood-clotting factors appeared during the evolution of vertebrates. In some cases, factors were lost during the evolution of some species, as was the case for factor XII for birds some three hundred million years ago.

Figure B-2 Evolutionary Tree of Blood Clotting outlines the evolution of representative pre-vertebrate and vertebrate species along a tree of life showing approximate dates of the introduction of key clotting factors over the five-hundred-million-year period. Evolution of the blood-clotting processes by natural selection has been able to meet the evolving design requirements of many different species, one species at the time, over this period of time.

A sample of the complexity, both in the number of steps and in the number of clotting factors and their interrelationship in the process is illustrated in Figure B-3 Human Blood Clotting Factors for the human clotting. Each of the many factors must work in a specific sequence for the clotting to occur properly. Details of the proteins and their activation that evolved in the clotting processes for various key species can be found in Doolittle's book.

The important summary observation is that the complex blood-clotting process observed in humans today evolved step-by-step from much simpler processes used by earlier, simpler life-forms by natural selection over hundreds of millions of years. Evolution by natural selection reflects changes made to meet the differing demands of each new species in the tree of life. The blood-clotting system was designed without a designer for each new species, of which there were thousands in the branches of the tree of human evolution. The blood-clotting system in man is just one of many complex systems which have evolved for humans.

Summary

D'Souza's and Zacharias's attempts to discredit Darwin's Theory and replace it by the Intelligent Design pseudo-science theory to explain the complexity of biological systems of humans should be rejected by all Christians, for evolutionary biological research has produced step-by-step, protein-by-protein descriptions of the evolution of complex biological systems, including two of the most complex, the human eye and vertebrate blood clotting. Further, no biological systems with irreducible complexity requiring the need for a supernatural Intelligent Designer have surfaced. Nature's processes have been able do the job of explaining biological evolution, however complex the systems may have become. Each step along the evolutionary path is explainable by Darwin's Theory.

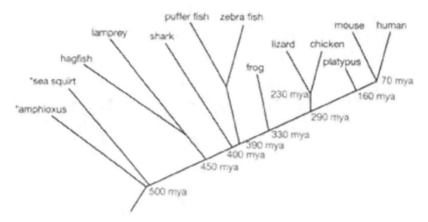

Figure 1 Human Tree of Life

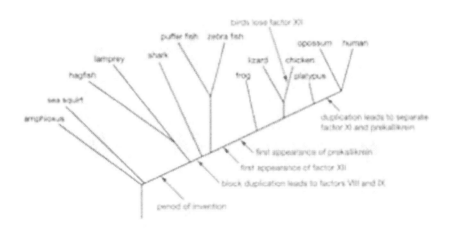

Figure 2 Evolutionary Tree of Blood Clotting

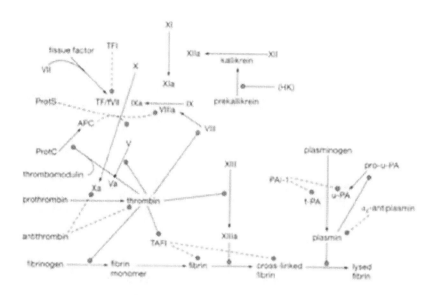

Figure 3 Human Blood Clotting Factors

Appendix C

Notes on *The Jefferson Bible*

THOMAS JEFFERSON, THE nation's third president, had the interest and drive to study many things. In doing so, he challenged many traditions of governments and religions of the time. To Jefferson no tradition was so sacred as to escape reconsideration in the light of new discoveries and the advances in knowledge.

> *The acts of Parliament, the English common law*
> *and the Bible itself must be read through the lens*
> *of enlightened human reason, then changed as*
> *reason might indicate.*

His library was the largest in the country at that time. It reflected his broad interest in philosophy and morality. He devoted a large section, with about 150 books, to what he called "moral philosophy." These books ranged from the early Greek philosophers Epicurus, Lucretius (with multiple copies of *De rerun natura*), and others to Spinoza, Voltaire, Toland, Hume, Locke, Bolingbroke, Priestly, and the Americans Ethan Allen and John Young. The Christian Bible was one of the books included.

He had studied the Bible on and off for years, and to add to his moral philosophy, he decided to extract Jesus's moral philosophy from the long Christian narrative, much of which he did not consider to be the words of Jesus. To find Jesus's core philosophy, he first dismissed the Old Testament and focused on the Gospels of the New Testament because he viewed Jesus as a reformer of the "*depraved religion of his own country.*" A hundred years before, the philosopher Spinoza had come to the same conclusion about the Bible and the contributions of Jesus contained in it.

In correspondence with Charles Thompson, Jefferson expressed his views on Jesus's philosophy, which he thought to assemble in a book:

> *His moral doctrines, relating to kindred and friends, were more pure and perfect than those of the most correct of the philosophers, and greatly more so than those of the Jews, and they went far beyond both in inculcating universal philanthropy, not only to kindred and fiends, to neighbors and countrymen, but to all mankind, gathering all into one family, under the bonds of love, charity, peace, common wants and common aids. A development of this head will evince the peculiar superiority of the system of Jesus over all others.*

He then proceeded to be a reformer of the New Testament. (Today he would be called a Progressive Christian.) Jefferson edited the New Testament in a rather straightforward manner. He used a pair of scissors and cut out passages he thought were Jesus's moral philosophy. He focused mainly on the parables and precepts, to which he added some chronological history of Jesus's life to link the pieces together. He then pasted the extracts into a blank book he titled *The Life and Morals of Jesus of Nazareth Extracted Textually from the Gospels in Greek, Latin, French and English.* He used four Bibles in four languages to be sure he got the translation to English correct. His little book honored what he thought were the "gems" of Jesus's moral philosophy, and he placed it in the "moral philosophy" section of his library alongside his collection of other moral philosophy books. This little book has become known as *The Jefferson Bible.*

Historians Henry Rubinstein and Barbara Clark Smith explain more about Jefferson's work:

> *Left out were those elements that he could not support with reason, that he believed were later embellishments, or what seemed superfluous or repetitious across the four Evangelists' accounts. Absent are the annunciations, the resurrection, the water being turned into wine, and the multitudes fed on five loaves of bread and two fishes. It essentially offers what the title indicates: a distillation of the teachings of Jesus the moral reformer, combined with what Jefferson accepted as the historical facts pertaining to Jesus the man.*

Martin Marty of the University of Chicago summarizes what Jefferson did:

> *In essence what Jefferson did was to remove the miracles and mystery and leave Jesus' moral philosophy which was contained in the parables, precepts and aphorisms. He made a Socrates out of Jesus.*

Gary Gutting, a Catholic from Notre Dame University, reached the same conclusion, albeit 212 years after Jefferson came to this observation in his little book:

> *The fundamental revelation is the moral ideal expressed in the biblical account of Christ's life. Whether or not that account is historically accurate, the New Testament Christ remains an exemplar of an impressive ideal.*

A modern critique of *The Jefferson Bible* by Laurel Gray, a retired Lutheran minister, reveals there are three questionable exceptions to the removal of miracles—two healing episodes and one reference to spirits. Jefferson must have considered these not supernatural:

- "He healed a man [with dropsy]."
- "Great multitudes followed him and he healed them there."
- "He gave them power over unclean spirits."

Today's biblical scholars believe that some passages relating to Jesus's history described in the New Testament are of questionable validity. However, these biblical scholars were not available to Jefferson, so he used the biblical passages as they were available to him.

What is not questionable is that Jefferson, an Atheist and Deist, reached out and documented his thoughts on the best of Christian philosophy for his own use and placed Jesus in the top ranks of contributors to the moral philosophy he used for his guidance.

Appendix D

Quiz on Atheists

Ten example statements on Atheists listed below are taken from the books by the Fundamentalist Christian writers D'Souza and Zacharias. These are formed as questions to engage the views of others. There are no right or wrong answers to the true/false questions. By answering the reader may find his/hers views relative to those of Fundamentalist Christians. The more statements you think are false the more your beliefs tend to be those of a Moderate or possibly a Progressive Christian. If you think they are all false then you may be an Atheist.

1. Atheists grasp nothing of eternal value, for they have no God. (True or False)
2. Atheists without God have no morality. (True or False)
3. Atheists believe morality is a dirty word, and immorality has no damning effect if it is kept in private. (True or False)
4. Atheists believe private practice and public practice are morally unrelated. (True or False)
5. Atheists believe that by the power of unaided reason, they can arrive at a satisfactory moral law. (True or False)
6. Atheists are spiritually dislodged, estranged from reason, and led into a delirium of vanity. (True or False)

7. Atheists recognize no law other than survival and are slaves of the moment. (True or False)

8. Atheists, having rejected God, flutter between pleasurable options, with inner peace eluding them. (True or False)

9. Hitler unintentionally exposed Atheism and forced it into its consequences. (True or False)

10. To be an intellectual is a great privilege, but to be an intellectual without God is dangerous. (True or False)

APPENDIX E

Defining the Wall of Separation

IN THE PAST fifty years, a number of Supreme Court rulings have been issued that further defines the legal status of the wall separating religion from government. Christian Fundamentalists regard several key court rulings as violating their biblical scriptures. Since these original rulings, numerous court cases have been brought against each ruling, and some cases modify the ruling. It can be expected that further legal cases will be brought before the Supreme Court, and new laws or modifications of existing ones could further define the wall of separation. These types of lawsuits continue today because of the intense interest by Fundamentalist Christians to have their God involved in the laws of the country. For example, although the *Roe v. Wade* case made it legal to have an abortion and a majority of Americans support a woman's rights to have an abortion, Fundamentalists continue to challenge the decision in the courtroom.

Brief summaries of seven past examples of Supreme Court rulings and one federal court ruling on the separation of church and state are listed:

1961—*Torcaso v. State of Maryland.* Court ruled that states could not compel officeholders to declare a belief or disbelief in a God. This overturned the Maryland's Constitution that said officials in the state of Maryland must believe in God to hold office.

1962—*Engle v. Vitale.* Religious prayers conducted by public school teachers violate the separation of church and state. An individual's right to pray is not in question.

1963—*Abington v. Schempp.* The Bible was judged to be a religious book and removed from use for religious instructions in public schools. Use of it in a historical context is permitted.

1973—*Roe v. Wade.* Abortion was made a legal medical procedure. Subsequent rulings have narrowed the abortion timing and procedures.

1980—*Stone v. Graham.* Display of the Ten Commandments was judged to be a religious symbol and not acceptable on public land and in public buildings. Use of the Christian Ten Commandments in a historical context is permitted.

1992—*Planned Parenthood v. Casey.* The court upheld the constitutional right of individuals to have an abortion but altered the standards of restrictions.

2005—*Kitzmiller v. Dover Area School District.* The plaintiffs successfully argued that Intelligent Design is a religious theory (creationism) and that the school board policy violated the Establishment Clause of the First Amendment to the US Constitution.

State courts have been increasingly used by Fundamentalist to contest laws which they believe conflict with Fundamentalist Christian values—particularly homosexual rights, birth control and gay marriages. It is expected these issues will be brought to the US Supreme Court in the near future.

INDEX

Endnotes

1 John Edward Terrell, *Evolution and the American Myth of the Individual*, New York Times, 2014

2 Susan Jacoby, *Freethinkers: A History of American Secularism*

3 Matthew Stewart, *Nature's God: The Heretical Origins of the American Republic*

4 Thomas Jefferson, *The Jefferson Bible: The Life and Morals of Jesus of Nazareth Extracted Textually from the Gospels in Greek, Latin, French and English*

5 Charles Blow, "Religious Constriction," *New York Times*, 2014

6 Gary Gutting, "Debating God: Notes on an Unanswered Question," *New York Times*, 2014

7 J. Riley-Smith, *The Crusades*, Yale University, 1987

8 Ravi Zacharias, *The Real Face of Atheism*

9 Lawrence Krauss, *A Universe from Nothing: Why There Is Something Rather than Nothing*

10 Jerry A. Coyne, "Stop Celebrating the Pope's Views on Evolution and the Big Bang," *New Republic*, 2014

11 Michael Novacek, "Prehistory's Brilliant Future," *New York Times*, 2014

12 Louis Perry, *Thank Evolution for God*, 2012

13 William Paley, *Natural Theology; or, Evidences of the Existence and Attributes of the Deity*, 1805

14 First name Last name, "The Challenge of Irreducible Complexity," *American Museum of Natural History*, 2002

[15] Gary Gutting, "Can Wanting to Believe Make Us Believers?," *New York Times*, 2014

[16] Paul MacLean, *The Triune Brain in Evolution*, 1990

[17] Patricia Churchland, *Brain-Wise: Studies in Neurophilosophy*

[18] Frans de Waal, *The Bonobo and the Atheist: In Search of Humanism among the Primates*

[19] Paul Churchland, *The Engine of Reason and the Seat of the Soul: A Philosophical Journey into the Brain*

[20] Patricia Churchland, *Braintrust: What Neuroscience Tells Us about Morality*

[21] William L. Shirer, *The Rise and Fall of the Third Reich*

[22] Gary Wills, *Papal Sin, Structures of Deceit*

[23] John Cornwell, *Hitler's Pope: The Secret History of Pius XII*

[24] John Barrow and Frank Tipler, *The Anthropic Principle*

[25] Stephen Hawking, *The Cambridge Lectures: Life Works*

[26] Laurence Krauss, *Atom: A Single Oxygen Atom's Odyssey from the Big Bang to Life on Earth*

[27] "Separation of Church and State," *Northwest Ordinance*, 2014

[28] Laurie Goodstein, *In Seven States, Atheists Push to End Largely Forgotten Ban*, New York Times, 2014

[29] Galileo, *Dialogue concerning the Two Chief World Systems*

[30] Dinesh D'Souza, *The Roots of Obama's Rage*

[31] Eric Michelsen, *Quirky Quantum Concepts*

[32] David Barash, "God, Darwin and My College Biology Class," *New York Times*, 2014

[33] Cambridge University, Biology Department, May 5, 2014, URL.

[34] Charles Darwin, *On the Origin of Species: By Means of Natural Selection*, 1859

[35] Trevor Lamb, "Evolution of the Eye," *Scientific American*, 2011

[36] George Johnson, "A Creationist's Influence on Darwin," *New York Times*, 2014

Made in the USA
Charleston, SC
18 February 2015